Paul and Third World Women Theologians

Loretta Dornisch

A Liturgical Press Book

THE LITURGICAL PRESS
Collegeville, Minnesota

The translations and paraphrases from the Bible are the author's.

Cover design by David Manahan, O.S.B. Photo by Annette Brophy, O.S.B. Art: Russian icon, St. Paul.

1   2   3   4   5   6   7   8

Library of Congress Cataloging-in-Publication Data
Dornisch, Loretta.
    Paul and third world women theologians / Loretta Dornisch.
        p.   cm.
    ISBN 0-8146-2553-3 (alk. paper)
    1. Bible.   N.T.   Epistles of Paul—Feminist criticism.
    2. Women theologians—Developing countries.   I. Title.
BS2650.2.D67   1999
227'.06'082—dc21   98-51061
                                                       CIP

Contents

Part Four: Major Theological Development for Rome

Introduction

What if the letters of Paul were written by Paula?

What difference would that make today? How would we read them? What if most of her co-workers were women? How would this change the traditions we have received? Would these letters then be more accessible to women and other oppressed groups throughout our broken world?

An exploration in reading and interpreting is worth our time to see how playing with the text may free us to make our own some new images, ideas, and stories needed for people today.

Readers are invited to bring imagination and stories to interact with the texts of Paula, with the texts of their own lives, and with the stories of oppressed peoples of the world. These will provide the perspectives for exploring the letters associated with Paul who called himself not only an apostle, one who was sent, but also a witness to the new life of resurrection. We will look first at selections from the beginnings, then from the development in major letters, and finally from the Letter to the Romans.

Themes of liberation and justice will emerge against a background of persons oppressing and oppressed, whether in the first century or in the twenty-first. A special emphasis will be given to the Third World whose women theologians are emerging as voices calling for a new consciousness. They speak for women who are often treated as less than human, and whose oppression can no longer be tolerated.

Although as women from economically developed cultures we cannot speak directly for women from the Third World, we can learn much from these women who have suffered so much and who are speaking out on behalf of those who seem to have no voice. Such conversation can be life-transforming; in fact, it can be conversion. If at the same time, we can hold a microphone for these voices to be heard, we will have performed a service.

To read the letters of Paul in dialogue with these women is a painful task. The pain comes from several sources. First is the pain of the women themselves as they cry out for life. Second is the pain of facing the patriarchal and oppressive cultural and religious aspects of Paul's letters. Third is the challenge of reading Paul against the experience of these women. Fourth is the difficulty of translating the death-resurrection insights of the first century into meaningful language for the twenty-first century. However, from the clash of world views there can also emerge intercultural understandings and, in fact, new life.

As sources for these new voices from around the globe, three books provide insights. The first is edited by Ursula King, *Feminist Theology from the Third World* (London: SPCK/Maryknoll, N.Y.: Orbis Books, 1994). The second is by Maria Pilar Aquino, *Our Cry for Life, Feminist Theology from Latin America* (Maryknoll, N.Y.: Orbis Books, 1993). The third is by Chung Hyun Kyung, *Struggle To Be the Sun Again, Introducing Asian Women's Theology* (Maryknoll, N.Y.: Orbis Books, 1990, 1994). It is hoped that these voices can continue to be heard loud and clear and that the twenty-first century can see redress of some of the wrongs and, in fact, a new world of full dignity for all women and for all oppressed persons.

A New Perspective

For many people today Paul needs a new perspective. He is sometimes seen as anti-woman, male-dominating, mired in images and concepts from ancient worlds some persons cannot relate to today. Yet why have his letters endured? Why do women in Guatemala, Nigeria, or Korea find a resonance in their experience today? Why has Paul continued to be a major resource for persons wanting to live a deep Christian life?

We shall explore some of these questions as we look at Paul's letters. Can we convert these texts to be woman-friendly, user-friendly, liberation-friendly?

Several perspectives or points of view will be helpful. First, we will hypothesize Paula as a co-worker, co-writer, co-thinker with Paul, even an alter-ego. This is not contradictory to the texts since Paul refers to at least three women as "co-workers" (Rom 16:3; Phil 4:3).

A second point of view will be that of various women named by Paul whether as co-workers or heads of households, or even as deacon or apostle. A third perspective will be that of imagined women of the first century with their various cultural and traditional world-views. The fourth perspective will be that of women today, from whatever continent, who are struggling to create life for themselves and others.

Most Bibles list fourteen letters associated with the traditions of Paul. Many scholars and others, on the basis of stylistic and content differences, agree on the major letters written by Paul: 1 Thessalonians, perhaps parts of 2 Thessalonians, 1 Corinthians, 2 Corinthians in some arrangements, Philippians, Philemon, Galatians, and Romans. Some see parts of letters grouped as one letter, for example, 2 Thessalonians and 2 Corinthians. Other letters are ascribed to followers of Paul: Colossians, Ephesians, Hebrews, and letters to Timothy and Titus. There are many excellent books which provide background, commentary, and discussion of these matters. Some are listed at the end of this book.

This commentary will presume the work of many women and men to whom we are indebted. But the thrust here will be in the tradition of reconstruction and of reflective commentary. In the ancient world something similar was sometimes called *midrash*.

The book is divided into several sections: Part One: Beginnings associated with the people of the large city of Thessalonica in northern Greece. Part Two: Developments associated with the people of Corinth, a major city for the growth of Christianity. Part Three: Themes connected with the people of Philippi and Galatia, now known as Asia Minor. Part Four: Major theological developments associated with a letter to the people of Rome. The later letters are not commented on here, although many of the themes appear in the letters which are considered.

We have then for our reflections a first perspective of Paula calling persons to faith, a second perspective of other women named by Paul, a third perspective of women of the first century, and a fourth perspective of women today, especially those from the so-called Third World. The reader is invited to interact with each of these perspectives in order to renew life for Christians today.

Part One: Beginnings

LETTERS TO THE THESSALONIANS

Thessalonica is a Greek city like New York, Rotterdam, or Hong Kong in that it is a crossroads and a port where many people from different cultures interact with each other. In Paul's time there was a large Jewish population. Paul was instrumental in founding there house churches of early Christians.

After going on to Athens and Corinth in about 51 of the Common Era (C.E.), he wrote a letter to the Christians in Thessalonica to encourage them in their active waiting for Christ to come.

We can picture him going to the market area of Corinth, the *agora*, and finding a scribe, a professional secretary, much as a business person today goes to a business center in a convention hotel to have a letter prepared. The scribe would probably take the dictation from Paul, writing on papyrus with a stylus, suggesting phrasing where appropriate. Paul would pay for the service.

On the other hand, it is possible that Paul made acquaintances who were scribes or who had scribal abilities, and who therefore could perform this service for Paul in a more private setting.

What about our hypothetical Paula? In the customs of the time, she would not usually be found in the public sector or in the *agora*. However, we can picture Paula in a house church as dictating to a scribe or suggesting phrases and ideas to Paul as the dictation unfolded, or as taking part in the lengthy discussions which preceded the writing of the letter.

Were other women involved in this process of discussion contributing to the composition of the letter? Yes. Sometimes the house church met in the dwelling owned or managed by a woman. These women may well have taken part in the discussions. Others mentioned as co-workers would also have made their contributions.

Does this happen today? Definitely. A letter today signed by one person is often the compilation of ideas and discussions to which many persons have contributed—whether it is a letter from a political figure such as a president, or a public letter printed in *The New York Times*. It is clear from Paul's letters that although he was a strong leader he interacted continually with many persons whom he influenced and who influenced him.

1 The First Letter to the Thessalonians:

Sufferings and Freedom

Paul begins what we call the First Letter to the Thessalonians with the structure he had learned as the appropriate form for beginning a letter:

> Paul and Silvanus and Timothy to the house church of the Thessalonians . . . (1 Thess 1:1).

But how does he think of this house church? It is an assembly, a gathering, only by reason of being in God-Father and in the Lord Jesus Christ. Why does Paul call God "Father"? Although "Father" is used in the Hebrew Bible to name God, the word becomes dominant in the Gospels. The prayer of Jesus addressing "Our Father" is a consistent part of the tradition of the New Testament. We are also reminded of the stories of the baptism and transfiguration of Jesus in which a voice from heaven speaks of Jesus as "beloved son" (Matt 3:17; 17:5; Mark 1:11; 9:7; Luke 3:22; 9:35). In John's Gospel Jesus is pictured as praying that his followers may be one as the Father and he are one (John 17:22). Paul has also received this "God as Father" tradition. The phrase is a consistent part of his prayer formulas at the beginning of each letter.

But Paul is not only from a Jewish culture. He is Greek speaking and familiar with Greek concepts and images. The Greek gods and any Greek father images are replaced by God the Father of Jesus, "God the Father of whom are all things" (1 Cor 8:6).

Parallel with "God-Father" is "Lord Jesus Christ" (1 Thess 1:1). "Jesus" is the name of the one associated with Paul's Damascus experience. Paul recognized and acknowledged Jesus as resurrected, as his Lord, and as the anointed one, the Christ, the Messiah.

What about our hypothetical Paula? Few women in that culture would ignore the accepted image of father. But for many then as today, "father" was a positive image of one who provides bread and other necessities, who cares for and respects, who indeed is a source of life. This seems to be the way Jesus perceived his father, so it is understandable that Paul, Paula, and other women of the first century would have found these connotations congenial. God as Father is source of life.

Some women today have difficulty with this language. For a variety of reasons "father" connotes for them domination, oppression, anti-woman qualities. These latter qualities are precisely what Paul and Paula reject as distortions of the Law and as characteristics from which Christ has freed them.

Parallel comments can be applied to the phrase "Lord Jesus Christ." Jesus is perceived precisely as the one who frees, as one who transcends the male-female category. The title "Lord" as "Mister" is an affirmation that Jesus is the Lord of Freedom, the one who leads into freedom, the one who transcends master-servant categories, the one who calls others friends. "Christ" is the anointed one, the one who comes to save from oppression, domination, or discrimination. To acknowledge Jesus as the provider of freedom is to give a human quality to the cosmos. Jesus emerges from a woman, a woman-child of simplicity, of the people, of the earth. Together they make human the gift of the earth, of the cosmos. The universe and the unnamable Other have a human face, a face that can smile or shed tears. In John's language, the Word has pitched a tent among us—in our flesh (John 1:14).

What is it that Paul, Paula, Silvanus, Silvana, Timothy, and Timothea send to the women, children, and men who live in Thessalonica? Two things: *charis,* the gift called "grace," and peace (1 Thess 1:1).

Next comes Paula's giving of thanks. This is the verb from which *eucharist* is taken. Its source is the daily giving of thanks in the Jewish prayer tradition. For the Christian assembly it transforms into the Christian giving of thanks in the eucharistic gatherings. What do Paula and the others give thanks for? For the Thessalonians. They pray for them, remember their *work* of faith and love and the endurance of their hope in the Lord who is named again as Jesus Christ in the presence of their God and Father (l Thess 1:3). They tell the persons:

> You are loved by God, you are chosen. The Good News came to you in power and in the Holy Spirit, a spirit of joy (1 Thess 1:4-6).

They have now turned from idols to serve instead a God who is alive and true (1 Thess 1:9). They are waiting for God's son, raised from the dead, Jesus, who frees us from the coming disasters *(orgēs)* (1 Thess 1:10).

What does this mean for women? Women are familiar with disasters, attributed to whatever source. Like those in earlier times, women today know too many women who die in childbirth, too many children who do not survive infancy, too many girl children who are sold into slavery, who are forced to work as child laborers, who are raped or given into oppressive marriages. In contrast, these women know they are called to faith, love, and hope. They are loved by God, given the joy of the Holy Spirit. In Jesus they find freedom.

1 Thess 2, 3

Many women from Africa, Central America, or Asia can relate to Paula's autobiographical allusions to her suffering and being shamefully treated (1 Thess 2:2), yet being bold or courageous in "our God" to speak the Good News "in much struggle." Women in Korea, in South Africa, in India are speaking out regarding the oppression of women and of the poor, whether this oppression is through prostitution aimed to serve tourists in Manila, or the oppression experienced by factory workers in Indonesia. They know they are not "as pleasing men" (1 Thess 2:4). They do not use "flattering words" (1 Thess 2:5). Like Paula, they are as "nurses cherishing their children, giving of their own souls" because the poor and oppressed are "beloved" to them (1 Thess 2:7-8). Those killing the prophets (1 Thess 2:15) and persecuting those who speak out have new names and faces, new nationalities. No wonder some look to a judgment and a coming of God or "the presence of our Lord Jesus Christ" (1 Thess 2:19) to give hope.

Such courage requires a faith not to be "moved by such affliction" (1 Thess 3:2, 3). As Paula was consoled by the faith of the Thessalonians and also by the support of Timothea in the first century, so women today are consoled by the support of others of like faith, whether it be a woman's movement in the Philippines against an unjust government, or a student group in Seoul clamoring for justice for oppressed factory workers. Such women know that paradoxically they live when they stand together in justice (1 Thess 3:8).

Paula prays for an increase of love toward one another and toward all (1 Thess 3:12):

> May your hearts be blameless in holiness before God and our Mother in the presence of Jesus (1 Thess 3:13), our liberator with all those in freedom.

1 Thess 4, 5

How are women to act today? Are they to follow the slavish interpretations of dominant colonial Christianity or cultural imperialism?

As women we experience regular and everyday discrimination: the limiting experiences of housewives confined to the home, as society assigns them to do; the despair of the wives who are beaten but who cannot separate from their husbands, "because of the children," because of social disapproval or because of emotional or psychological dependence on their husbands. There exist the exploitation, discrimination and sexual harassment of our sisters who work either in the rural areas as invisible contributions to agricultural production or in an urban setting as factory workers. We know about the continuous insult to our womanhood in the mass media, in advertisements and the more blatant exploitation of our sisters in prostitution, mail-order brides, etc. (Kyung, 87).

Are women to be silent in the face of such injustice? Are they to "obey" in a false sense of kowtowing to exploitive authority? Today, Asian women, African women, American women are saying "No." Like those in Thessalonica, they are not to be accomplices in fornication, in lust, in fraud. On the contrary, women are called to wholeness through a spirit of holiness, the spirit that comes from God. "You yourselves are taught by God to love one another" (1 Thess 4:9).

In the first century Paul urged these early Christians to "be quiet, to practice your own things, to work with your own hands" (1 Thess 4:11). If by this Paul meant not to upset people, not to rock the boat, some may think this is understandable in the context of the times. Jews were persecuted, generally lived in what we today call ghettoes, were even expelled from Rome. Women today face a like tension. Even in business, can one be effective if one "rocks the boat"? On the other hand, how much can one keep quiet without compromising one's integrity?

It is interesting, too, that submission does not seem to be the road Paul usually took. In fact, because he spoke out, he was beaten, imprisoned, and even expelled from cities. Perhaps we have misinterpreted this directive. The last lines urge "that you walk becomingly toward those who are outside so that you may have need of nothing" (1 Thess 4:12). This is precisely what women are finding it necessary to do: to assume an independence so they can work with their own hands, articulate their own ideas, and be neither co-dependent nor dependent in ways that compromise their own integrity. If this means changing or ending a relationship or a job, they are finding the courage to take the necessary steps.

In her view, Paula had seen the resurrected Christ on the road to Damascus. She had also absorbed from the cultural milieu the concept of a world coming to an end. Women, too, according to the Gospel accounts, had seen the resurrected Christ. For most, many "worlds" had ended. By the year 70 C.E., Jerusalem, with many Jewish people, was destroyed.

We are reminded of the situation in Guatemala where at least one hundred thousand persons have been killed, and where everyone can tell of family or friends who have "disappeared." In her powerful narrative Rigoberta Menchû, Nobel peace prize winner, tells her own account of such deaths and disappearances (Rigoberta Menchû, *I, Rigoberta Menchû: An Indian Woman in Guatemala*, edited and introduced by Elisabeth Burgos-Debray, London: Verso, 1984). People of Argentina, Chile, and other Latin American countries tell similar stories.

If we focus on Bosnia, we hear the stories of rapes and murders beyond counting. In such situations, one may speak easily of the end of the world. An awareness of the continuing threat of nuclear, ecological, or military destruction makes very real the possibility of the end of the world as human beings think of it. In Christian terms, one can use the language of the second coming to articulate a hope for judgment, reconciliation, and/or a new world.

Paula links the images to a belief that "Jesus died and rose again" and that those who remain or "those who died in Christ will rise again . . . and so we shall always be with the Lord" (1 Thess 4:14-17).

Some women in Korea, Africa, or Bosnia, like the women in Thessalonica, comfort each other with these words (1 Thess 4:18). Others find the language too fundamentalist, yet can transform the images into hope of a new era which they may be helping to create.

Women then and now experience the darkness, the wars, famines, and dislocations. They know the "Day of the Lord" can come as a "thief in the night" or as the "birth pains of a woman pregnant with child." But such women in another way are not in darkness but "children of light, children of the day." Such women are called to watch, to wear faith, love, and hope, in the hope of wholeness in Jesus Christ, of living together with Christ (1 Thess 5:2-10). For such women, Christ transcends male and female, not to ignore sexuality, but to embrace the richness of both. A spirit of holiness calls these women to joy always, to pray without ceasing, to be at peace. The one who calls them and who empowers them is faithful (1 Thess 5:24).

2 The Second Letter to the Thessalonians:

Responsibility and Evil

2 Thess 1

Paula's Second Letter to the Thessalonians centers on the mystery of evil. Whether it is one letter or several put together, whether it comes from Paul's time or later, it reflects times of persecution and evil that are beyond the rational.

The women who experienced mass rapes in Bosnia, the women walking the roads of Africa in the hope of escaping war or famine must raise questions about evil, about vengeance, and about justice. Is there a God who will "repay those who are afflicting you?" (2 Thess 1:6). In the context of the holocaust, Elie Wiesel decided it is too hard to name a God who could allow the holocaust. Paula in the first century resorts to "flaming fire" and "everlasting destruction" for those who work evil, "who do not know God and who do not obey the Good News of Jesus" (2 Thess 1:8-9). Those who read this in a literal sense find an easy "justice" in such expectations. In contrast to the vengeance, they see the "good" and perhaps themselves "counted worthy" of the kingdom of God (2 Thess 1:5).

Many others are equally horrified by the evils, but they see a complexity that doesn't seem to appear in this letter. While affirming individual responsibility, they nevertheless recognize a complexity of society and of individuals that doesn't easily place blame.

The early Christians, like the Jews, were often persecuted for what they believed. They had found in a new way of life a simplicity, a call to faith and love that was countercultural, to say the least. If they were persecuted for following this call, they felt that somehow Christ was thereby "glorified" in them (2 Thess 1:12). They were not to be shaken in mind or disturbed by a spirit, a work, or even by a false letter that the "day of Christ is at hand" (2 Thess 2:2).

2 Thess 2

Here we have a movement away from the imminent coming described in 1 Thessalonians. Now a "son of perdition" (2 Thess 2:3) is to come first. The context seems to suggest the horrors of the destruction of Jerusalem in 70 C.E. and the violation of the Temple.

The problem of evil is not resolved. Evils beyond explanation abound. Paula calls those to whom she writes to "stand firm, hold the traditions you have been taught" (2 Thess 2:15). "Our Lord Jesus Christ and God our Father have loved us and given us the strength of the ages and a good hope by grace" (2 Thess 2:16).

2 Thess 3

Paula asks that the Word of the Lord may run freely in her and that "we may be delivered from perverse and evil men" (2 Thess 3:1-2).

> May the Lord direct your hearts into the love of God and into the patience of Christ (2 Thess 3:5).
>
> Do not lose heart doing good (2 Thess 3:13).
>
> May the Lord of peace give you peace (2 Thess 3:16).

Women today often feel impelled to call for vengeance, both for wrongs done to them as well as for the horrors perpetrated on their sisters around the world. While this may be understandable, women such as those writing as Asian women theologians are calling instead for a new hope and a new truth which names the horrors, which refuses to cooperate with them or ignore them, and which works through education, politics, cultural change, and spirituality to help women find the freedom of Christ for themselves and for others.

Part Two:
Major Developments

LETTERS TO THE CORINTHIANS

1 The First Letter to the Corinthians:

Strife, Community, and the Body of Christ

1 Cor 1, 3

Like Thessalonica, Corinth was a somewhat cosmopolitan city. Its nearby port of Cenchrae, its position on major routes, and its major cult places made it a crossroads where many people passed through. The church at Corinth became a major assembly of those "called saints" (1 Cor 1:2).

Paula sees herself as a "called apostle through the will of God," in other words, one sent to them by God (1 Cor 1:1). Paula is grateful for the gifts they have received from God, gifts of speech and knowledge (1 Cor 1:4-5). They also are waiting for the coming of the Lord Jesus Christ (1 Cor 1:7). Nevertheless as some from Chloe reported, there are strifes among them (1 Cor 1:11). Paula urges them to be joined together in the same mind (1 Cor 1:10). From the next letter to the Corinthians, and from a later letter from Clement to the Corinthians, we know that these contentions continued.

For church groups today, this is very disturbing but at the same time very consoling. Strife seems unfortunately to be part of the human condition, even in church groups. We like to think that persons in a like faith love each other and avoid strife. We are indeed called to that kind of love, but it does not come easily and dissension is always a scandal. We think of Rosa Parks walking to work for a year because other Christians denied her right to sit in an open seat on the bus. We think of women martyred in El Salvador because they named as unjust the killing and the disappearances of husbands and brothers. We think of women denied access to certain ministries by reason of their being women. In spite of our prayers, we are still scandalized by the oppression of women in churches, in business, in government, and in many other aspects of society. Paula asks: "Is Christ divided?" (1 Cor 1:13). The power of Christ is not in the wisdom of this world (1 Cor 1:20). Paula preaches Christ crucified which is the power and wisdom of God (1 Cor 1:23-24).

> Don't you know that you are the temple of God and that the spirit of God dwells in you? (1 Cor 3:16).

1 Cor 4–5

Women who are misjudged can appropriate to themselves the images Paul and others learned through experience:

> So let a man reckon us
> as attendants of Christ
> and stewards of mysteries of God . . .
>
> It is a very small thing
> if I am judged by you . . .
> the one judging me is the Lord . . .
>
> We are fools because of Christ . . .
> We hunger and thirst,
> are naked and are beaten . . .
>
> We work with our own hands.
>
> When we are reviled we bless.
> When we are persecuted, we endure.

When we are defamed, we entreat.
We are made as the refuse of this world (1 Cor 4:1, 3-4,
    10, 11-13).

Whether they are battered women in the United States, political prisoners in Tibet, or Korean women told to keep their place, women are being called to step out, to name the evils, to refuse to be denied their call to a full humanity. They are refusing to cooperate with oppressive social structures. They are applying the active, articulating, non-violence discovered in the political activism of this century, and thereby freeing themselves.

Paula speaks many words to condemn fornication in the Corinthian church. Women around the world affirm Paula's naming of the sexual exploitation that goes on in rural areas, in urban areas, in the hiddenness of suburban life. Exploitation may include the Catholic young women in Manila's brothels of the tourist industry, or the mistresses used as part of the cultural system by unfaithful South American upper-class husbands, or the women in North American cities who finally recognize the infidelity of their profligate partners and who move toward divorce. In any of these situations fornication is recognized as oppression at the deepest levels of misuse.

But today we want to ask, "How did the women in the first century hear these words?" The fornicators were condemned in the strongest language, even to the point of punishment and excommunication. But who were the women who are not mentioned? Were they the prostitutes of the time, temple prostitutes condoned in the name of religion, or prostitutes associated with brothels such as that excavated along the marble street of Ephesus? Or were they single women who were then ostracized for a lifetime of alienation? Or were they married women compromising their own marriages, or widows dependent on income from outside sources?

The situation named by Paula is one "not so much as named among the nations, that one should have his father's wife" (1 Cor 5:1). The cultural context makes this an even greater affront to women. The violation is presented not primarily as that of the woman, but of the father whose authority and property rights are violated by the son.

What can we say of a woman violated by her own son, or by some other person in a similar relationship? Without denying the possible collaboration of the woman, we nevertheless have to ask what brokenness of the human condition and of society makes possible such aberrations from the expected norms? What was the freedom called for by Christ and preached by Paula, which would contradict such exploitation and oppression?

What Paula called for is what women call for today. In homey images which refer to the background of the exodus flight from Egypt and its celebration in the feast of Passover, Paula links Christ to the Passover "sacrificed for us" (1 Cor 5:7).

> Purge out the old leaven
> that you may be a new lump
> as you are unleavened.
>
> For indeed our Passover was Christ.
> So let us keep feast
> —not with old leaven
> —not with leaven of malice or of evil
> —but with the unleavened bread
>   of sincerity and truth (1 Cor 5:7-8).

In the Jewish context, "old leaven" is that which contaminates. It lacks the purity of new beginnings, of being on the road out of slavery into freedom and simplicity. Passover signifies movement from oppression into spring and new life.

The word "Passover" in Hebrew is *pesach*. Although we appropriately translate it "Passover," the origins and meaning are obscure. One of the possibilities of its basic meaning is "dance," the dance of freedom and festivity.

Christ is the new dance, the new Passover. We are called to celebrate not with the old leaven which Paula interprets as the leaven of malice and evil, but with the unleavened bread now linked with sincerity and truth. The word translated "sincerity" suggests a lack of artificiality, with no attempt to deceive or pass off as genuine what is artificial. "Truth" tears away any veil or covering.

These are the traits women are calling for: simplicity, lack of pretense, truthfulness to the dignity of each human being, a dance of freedom and festivity. But these are not the qualities most women experience. Whether in business, in government, in church structures, in family, women too often experience the opposite: coverups, pretense, lack of dignity, lack of respect, lack of freedom. In Christ who defies oppressive conventions, they see a model who points the way and gives hope.

Fornicators are not the only problem in the Corinthian church. Others are named as coveters, as idol worshipers, as railers, drunkards, or rapists (1 Cor 5:9-10). Though the acts are various, they all partake of the same hypocrisy, disrespect, and oppression. They all distort the simplicity and freedom of human dignity. Paula concludes: "Remove the evil one out of yourselves" (1 Cor 5:13). This no doubt is rightly translated to indicate excommunication from the community.

Christians today who read the Gospel have difficulty with this because Jesus is known as one who feasted with "sinners," as one open to interaction with all persons, as one calling such persons to conversion and new life.

This tension is a difficult one for individuals and communities. In the communities described by Paula, the rapists, fornicators, drunkards, and idol worshipers are evidently such threats to the community that the community's very life is threatened. No doubt individuals, especially women, are also severely threatened by such persons. What is the community to do?

Individuals and communities today are threatened with the same difficulties. Should a woman frequently raped by her husband remain in that situation? Most people today would say "No." Not only her dignity, but her life as a woman is threatened. But where are the supports, social or economic, for her to confront or escape such oppression?

Even intentional faith communities are often threatened with lust or rape, under the guise of Christian love. How difficult it is to work for the common good and the good of the individuals involved without succumbing to the same kind of temptations the Corinthian community experienced. We may also apply "Remove the evil one out of yourselves" (1 Cor 5:13) to that violent and oppressive part of each of us. Jesus said, "Judge not and you shall not be judged" (Matt 7:1; Luke 6:37). We can judge the action, whether of individuals or of societies, but to read the interior or to be ignorant of the complexities of motives and the responsibilities within complex societal structures is usually impossible. To work for healing, to call to healing, to bring tough love is the challenge.

1 Cor 6

Paula calls the followers of Christ to reject such oppressive sins of the body because

> You are washed,
> you are made holy,
> you are made just
> in the name of the Lord Jesus Christ
> and by the Spirit of our God (1 Cor 6:11).

> The body is not for fornication
> but for the Lord
> and the Lord for the body.
> God both raised the Lord
> and will raise us up
> through his power.
> Don't you know that your bodies
> are members of Christ? (1 Cor 6:13-15).

> Don't you know that your body
> is the temple or shrine

of the Holy Spirit
who is in you?
You have the Holy Spirit from God
and you are not your own.
You were bought with a great price.
Then praise God in your body (1 Cor 6:19-20).

Most middle-class women don't usually think of themselves as being "bought"—even with a great price. However, most women of the world are very much aware that their bodies can not only be bought, but can be bought very cheaply. Worse yet, in some places, a girl child's body is not only cheap, but it is such a liability that a female child is aborted or immediately killed at birth. In these days when cost effectiveness is a primary value, having a child is a huge financial commitment, whether the costs are paid by parents or by a government. The cost of health care is another indication of the financial contexts of our bodies.

How startling and affirming then is the language that we are "bought with a great price." Women are of infinite value. The preaching, healing, and suffering of God's child Jesus demonstrate the infinite worth of a woman. Not only that, but a woman is a shrine, a temple of the Holy Spirit, the Spirit of God. Such respect and dignity are beyond what any culture previously has called forth.

The women in the first centuries understood what a radical concept this is. No wonder they felt called to be Christians. Women through the ages and today also recognize the respect and dignity to which they are called. They are not meant to be sex objects or toys. They are one with the God of the universe.

1 Cor 7

Continuing problems for the people of Corinth concerned marriage and other relationships. Although we sometimes pretend otherwise, such problems are universal. Many societies posit a basic relationship between a man and a woman as well as the interrelationships which follow for the families involved. Many cultures have extended family structures. Some are matriarchal explicitly or implicitly. Among the former are certain Iroquois tribes; among the latter are some African-American families. More dominant today as well as in the first century are patriarchal structures in which the male is dominant.

Neither Jesus nor Paul could culturally jump two thousand years to see the variety of relationships lived today. In the light of the patriarchal worlds of which they were part, it is even more remarkable that they critiqued the marriage customs of their times, that they advocated human values over oppressive laws or customs, and that they held out freedom as necessary for human dignity. In this way Jesus is pictured by Matthew's church as defending the position of woman against a man's divorcing her as was permitted by Moses. Jesus equalizes male and female as one flesh (Matt 19:3-7). He acknowledges various kinds of relationships (Matt 19:10-12). Apparently, he remains single.

In his turn, Paul as he describes himself evidently is not married. Since he expects the coming Day of the Lord, he urges the unmarried and widows to remain as such (1 Cor 7:8), but he acknowledges the diversity of marriage relationships and that a difference of belief between wife and husband may lead to separation (1 Cor 7:11-16). "As God has called each, so let him walk" (1 Cor 7:17).

Similar common sense as Paul understands it is applied to arguments over circumcision (1 Cor 7:18-20), slavery (1 Cor 7:21-23), virginity (1 Cor 7:25-28), and food offered to idols (1 Cor 8).

1 Cor 8–10

How are women to reflect on these concerns today? Many today hold as ideal a lifetime relationship of one woman and one man in Christ. Other women and some men began with that ideal but find themselves in a broken or oppressive marriage. Their journey has led to divorce.

In some African tribal cultures, a prevailing structure includes a man with three or four wives. To become a Christian and to observe Christian marriage laws is to do grave injustice by abandoning these women to a non-family structure and to economic poverty. The son of one such married man is a convert to Roman Catholicism and a bishop. He asks what Jesus would advise his father. What is just? Certainly not to abandon the women. In another context an African woman theologian pleads with African men to be as compassionate as Joseph was with Mary when faced with inappropriate laws or customs.

Many African women theologians and Christian witnesses can say with new meaning:

Am I not free?
Am I not an apostle, one who is sent?
Have I not seen Jesus Christ our Lord?
Are you not my work in the Lord? (1 Cor 9:1).

To claim the Gospel is to claim this kind of freedom. Paul understood this. Paula understood this. The women in the early Christian communities rejoiced to have such freedom in Christ proclaimed. And so do many women today. All are called to oneness in Christ. Such oneness is reinforced and actualized by sharing in the bread and wine.

The cup of blessing
 which we bless—
Is it not communion
 of the blood of Christ?

The bread which we break—
Is it not communion
 of the body of Christ? (1 Cor 10:16).

These two questions have the quality of a formula of the early Christians, or perhaps even a hymn with a

cross or chiastic structure, placing words and sounds
in such a way that they can easily be learned and re-
membered. They indeed connote more than the simplicity of indicative sentences.

"Cup" is *potērion,* a cup which includes the drink.
But this is not just a cup or drink like any other cup or
drink; it is the cup of blessing. This is the cup of covenant or relationship in the Jewish tradition of Sabbath,
of meals, and of Exodus. It is also the cup of inheritance, heritage, or family. It links the tradition to the origins of the creation of the universe and the creation of
a human family, of relationships and contracts formed
for aeons, and that will continue for aeons.

"Bread" is *arton,* the loaf of presence linked with
the same traditions as the cup, but also making new the
tradition of bread from the Exodus, from the ancient
feast of Unleavened Bread which preceded David by
thousands of years, and from the twelve loaves of freshly
baked bread in the Temple which signified the presence
of God for the Hebrews.

The naming and the actions are paralleled:

> We bless the cup.
> We break the bread.

"Cup" and "bread," "bless" and "break" are united
by assonance, the relishing of similar sounds. In the
same way "blood" and "body" are united by consonan-
tal and vowel sounds of *a, m, t,* and *o.* In each case it is
the blood of *Christ,* the body of *Christ. Estin* as a verb
of *being* or *predication* embraces the words of "blood
of Christ" and "body of Christ."

What does this mean for women? Women share in
this cup of blessing. They share in the covenant, the
tradition of Sabbath, of meals, and of Exodus. Women
share in the inheritance, heritage, and family, of the fullness of the creation of the universe and the creation of
the human family. By reason of their continuing to give
birth and to nourish physically, culturally, and spiritually women are bodily bearers of the cup of blessing. It

was a woman's blood which gave birth and life to Abraham and Sarah, to Moses and Miriam, to David, Michal, and Bathsheba, to Jesus and Mary. It is woman who will continue this inheritance of blood into the next centuries and into the aeons to come.

With the Lord of creation, woman creates body, the body of Abraham or Sarah, the body of Moses or Miriam, the body of David, Michal, or Bathsheba, the body of Jesus or Mary. The body is nourished from her own body and then from the bread or from whatever food is basic to her culture. We even shape bread in the form of a body. In some cultures "breadfruit" is perceived to resemble the human body. A bowl of rice is a bowl of life.

Women understand the blessing of the cup of blessing as communion. Each evening as Hebrew women bless the Sabbath cup, they bring family and friends together united with the human family in the context of the cosmos. The word for "communion" in Greek is *koinonia,* a "fellowship," a "womanship," a community. This is a word that became special to the early Christians as they found community they had not experienced before and as they found oneness in the Christ.

> For we many are
> one bread, one body,
> for we all partake
> of the one bread (1 Cor 10:17).

How exciting, but how natural, for women to consider all as one bread, one body, whether Anglo, Hispanic, African-American, Asian, Latin American, or African. The grain may differ, the color may reflect different shades, but food is basic to the human body. Woman knows this and recognizes the oneness.

1 Cor 11

Paul has a discourse on relationship that many women today find offensive (1 Cor 11:1-17). Can Paula do something with this? The usual translation begins: "Be imitators of me as I am of Christ" (1 Cor 11:1).

Part of the problem lies in the word for "imitators"— *mimetai. Mimesis* in Greek thought suggests a reflection that is also reality of relationship. Greek drama can so reflect human experience that drama and experience become one. This can be the experience of persons in liturgy, in which liturgical action and the persons participating become one, and even move into a future together. Paula is saying of herself, then, that she reflects Christ and her reflection affects Christ so that a oneness is the result. To ask others to enter into this *mimesis,* then, is to ask that the radiance and interaction be extended.

More difficult is the description of Christ as the head of the man and the man as the head of the woman. But the head of Christ is God (1 Cor 11:3). Perhaps Paul is being careless in his analogies. Perhaps he too easily follows a discourse on "head" because he moves on to dictate that men should pray with heads uncovered (1 Cor 11:7), and women should pray and prophesy with heads covered. "Aren't we strange creatures," says Paula, "that we carry culture to such an extreme?"

More understandable and more contemporary is the condemnation of divisions, whether these be doctrinal or related to class (1 Cor 11:18-22). How can some be hungry and others full and yet come together for the Lord's supper? The bread of the Lord's supper must be related to the hunger of the world, including those close among us who are hungry.

Paula then includes the formula shared by the early Christians:

> For I received from the Lord
> what I also gave to you,
> that the Lord Jesus
> in the night in which he was betrayed
> took bread
> and having given thanks
> broke and said:

"This is my body for you.
Do this for my remembrance."

In a similar way
after supper
he took the cup saying:
"This cup is the new covenant
in my blood.
Do this as often as you drink
for my remembrance."

For as often as
you eat this bread
and drink the cup
you announce the death of the Lord
until he comes (1 Cor 11:23-26).

Women too have received this tradition. They take to themselves this body given for them. They drink this cup of the new covenant. They do this in remembrance of Christ and to announce his death until he comes.

Since in many cultures and church traditions women are not welcome at the table of men, they respond in diverse ways. Some, like the woman who anointed the feet of Jesus, ignore custom and go directly to the Christ. Others unite together not unlike the group mentioned in Luke 8 as ministering to them. They take responsibility for themselves and act as a group of women. They can remember the saying of Jesus: "Where two or three are gathered in my name, there I am in their midst" (Matt 18:20).

Other women perceive a table which excludes them as unacceptable. In fact, they can apply to those who exclude them:

Let a man prove himself
and so eat of the bread
and drink of the cup (1 Cor 11:28).

Whoever eats the bread
or drinks the cup of the Lord unworthily
will be guilty
of the body and blood of the Lord (1 Cor 11:27).

So if the poor are excluded, if women are excluded, if persons are excluded by reason of color or culture, the remembrance of the Lord's supper is distorted and makes those responsible "guilty of the body and blood of the Lord."

1 Cor 12

Working toward justice does not preclude diversity of gifts. It is the Spirit of God, a Holy Spirit, that enables persons to say "Jesus is Lord" (1 Cor 12:3).

> There are differences of gifts
>   but the same Spirit.
> There are differences of ministries
>   and the same Lord.
>
> There are differences of works
>   but the same God
>   working all things in all (1 Cor 12:4-6).

What are some of these gifts? A word of wisdom, a word of knowledge, faith, cures, power, prophecy, discerning of spirits, kinds of tongues or speech, interpretation of tongues. But all are one and the same Spirit (1 Cor 12:8-11).

Paula then uses the analogy of the oneness and the interrelationships within the body as a symbol of the body of Christ.

> The body is one but has many members.
> By one Spirit we were all baptized
>   into one body,
>   whether Jews or Greeks,
>   whether slaves or free (1 Cor 12:12-13).

And women add:

> whether women or men.

Foot, hand, ear, eye—all are interworking members of the body. Who are the members of the body of Christ who are integral to its working:

women, men, children;
Africans, Asians, Anglos,
Latinos, Euros, Aborigines,
poor, middle, rich,
smart, deprived, learning. . . .

Whatever the cultural or economic diversity, all are members of the body of Christ. As Paula humorously points out: "Where would be the hearing if the whole body were an eye?" (1 Cor 12:17).

There should be no division
  in the body.
The members should give
  the same care to one another (1 Cor 12:25).

If one member suffers,
  all suffer.
If one member is honored,
  all rejoice (1 Cor 12:26).

But what is the best gift?

1 Cor 13

Paula's great hymn about love may well have been created by a group of women. We do not know its source. Its rhythm and poetic language suggest it was originally sung or chanted. It is a masterpiece of world literature.

Women should not be taken in by fancy "tongues, whether human or angelic" (1 Cor 13:1). Other gifts, no matter how impressive—such gifts as "prophesying, understanding all mysteries, having such faith as to move mountains—if I have these—without love, I am nothing" (1 Cor 13:2).

What about good actions? "If I distribute all my goods, if I give my body to be burned—if I don't have love, I am nothing" (1 Cor 13:3).

How does love act?
Love makes long sacrifices.

Love is kind, the way Christ is kind:
   chrestenetai (1 Cor 13:4).

What does love not do?
Love is not jealous.
Love does not vaunt itself,
   is not puffed up
   does not act unbecomingly,
   does not seek things for herself,
   is not provoked,
   does not calculate evil,
   does not rejoice over wrong,
   but rejoices with the truth,
   covers all things,
   believes all things,
   hopes all things,
   endures all things (1 Cor 13:4-7).

Love never fails—
   If there are prophecies,
      they will be abolished.
   If there are tongues,
      they will cease.
   If there is knowledge,
      it too will be abolished (1 Cor 13:8).

For we know in part
and we prophesy in part
But when the fullness comes
that in part will be abolished (1 Cor 13:9-10).

When I was an infant
   I spoke as an infant,
   I thought as an infant,
   I reasoned as an infant.

When I became adult,
   I abolished the things of the infant (1 Cor 13:11).

Yet we see
   through a mirror
      in an enigma,
   but in the fullness
      we see face to face.

Yet I know in part
   but in the fullness
      I shall know fully
      as I am fully known.

For now there remain
   faith, hope, love,
      these three,

but the greatest of all is Love (1 Cor 13:12-13).

Women and Jesus learned these lessons from each other just as women in Guatemala today learn these lessons from their families and from the example of Jesus. Jesus preached and lived a life of love. It was his example with the woman who loved much (Luke 7:47), and with his story of the Samaritan who lived the two great commandments of love (Luke 10:25-37). It was his example of loving them to the giving of his life, who loved them even unto the end (John 13:1), that inspired them to a new kind of love that was selfless and uncalculating. This is not a love of false victimhood, too often preached to the destruction of women. This is a love of full dignity, of equal to equal, of adult to adult.

1 Cor 14

In contrast to this beautiful hymn is a discourse on "tongues." This phenomenon in the early Church which is renewed in charismatic groups throughout the centuries and which continues today is often accompanied by disputes over how to interpret these sounds sung in "other languages" or more typically in sounds and syllables not recognized as a known language. Attributed to the Holy Spirit, the proclaiming requires an interpreter who explains what the Holy Spirit is saying through this speech. According to Paul, the gift is easily abused and leads to confusion rather than peace (1 Cor 14:33).

The direction in 1 Cor 14:34-35 is a contradiction to the prevailing thrusts of Paula's letters: "Let women keep silence in the assemblies . . ." Some suggest

Paula is only reflecting customs of the times such as prevailed in many synagogues. Others insist these words are such a contradiction of the Christianity preached by Paula that they must have been inserted by another author. Whatever the discussion, such words are not only contrary to Paula's dictum that

> in Christ
> there is neither Jew nor Greek,
> there is neither slave nor free,
> there is not male and female,
> but all are one in Christ (Gal 3:28).

But they are contradictory to the example and teaching of Jesus found in the Gospels: Jesus, who associated with women, treated them as equals and called them to freedom. It should be noted that direction was also given to men who spoke in tongues that if there were no interpreter

> let him keep silence in the assembly
> and let him speak to himself and to God (1 Cor 14:28).

"Let all things be done becomingly and according to order" (1 Cor 14:40) shows that too often things were not done "becomingly" and "according to order." Indeed, the contradiction testifies to the fact that women did speak in tongues.

Subsequent letters by Paula and others show that the matter was not settled easily, that the phenomenon of tongues with its associated problems continued and that women continued to speak in spite of this slavish dictum to the contrary. They had heard and they hear the message of Christ and the primary message of Paula.

1 Cor 15

Paula's various instructions lead up to the climax of Paula's belief:

For I handed on to you
among the first things
what I also received:

that Christ died
on behalf of our sins
according to the Scriptures
and that he was buried
and that he has been raised
on the third day
according to the Scriptures,

and that he was seen by Cephas,
then by the twelve;
afterwards he was seen
by over five hundred at one time;

of these most remain until now
though some fell asleep (died);
afterward he was seen by James
then by all the apostles
and last of all
he was seen by me
as one snatched out of the womb.

For I am the least
   of the apostles
I am not sufficient
   to be called an apostle
because I persecuted
   the gathering of God
   but by the grace of God
   I am what I am . . . (1 Cor 15:3-10).

But we have to ask: where is the consistent gospel tradition of the women at the tomb who first saw the resurrected Christ and who took the word of their experience and proclaimed it to others including the twelve and Peter (Cephas)? Is Paul reflecting a male-dominated assembly tradition that ignores women, denies their existence by reason of their gender, and too easily has fallen into the patriarchal, classist, sexist society which Jesus critiqued and confronted in his actions, in his parables, and in his teachings?

Beginning with verse five we would have to rewrite in order better to reflect the Good News of Jesus:

> and that he was seen by Mary Magdalen
> and by Joanna and Mary of James
> and by the other women who were with them
> who told the apostles these things (Luke 24:10).

> Now when Jesus was risen
>   early the first day of the week
> he appeared first to Mary Magdalen . . . (Mark 16:9).

> And the angel said to the women . . .
> Going quickly tell his disciples
> that he is risen from the dead . . . (Matt 28:5, 7).

> Jesus said to her, Mary . . .
> go to my brothers . . . (John 20:16, 17).

Even though the gospel resurrection stories were probably written later than the First Letter to the Corinthians, the latter needs to be corrected by the consistent gospel tradition of Mary Magdalen and the other women. It is not enough to say that Paul is listing those males who can be recognized officially as witnesses and as authorities. The witness and the resurrection authority are given to Mary Magdalen and the other women.

This is the witness and resurrection authority that women of the Third World are claiming as their own. They are recognizing and naming the indignities and injustices of male-dominated societies, churches, and traditions. They know that Jesus does not call them to accept rape and prostitution as the norm, that Jesus does not call them to tolerate beatings from their husbands, that Jesus does not condone the mutilation of their genitals, that Jesus who said "Let the little children come to me" (Matt 19:14; Mark 10:14; Luke 18:16) is irate at the sight of infants killed because they are female. They are reading anew the tradition and they are writing it in their blood in the hope of a resurrection both now and in the future.

These women today may well say with Paula:

By the grace of God
I am what I am
and her gift to me
was not empty
but I worked harder
than all of them
yet not I,
but the grace of God with me (1 Cor 15:10).

These women proclaim that Christ has been raised (1 Cor 15:12) and by reason of that resurrection they expect a continuing resurrection to dignity, to freedom, and to a fullness of life that are signs of a continuing life of the ages. Only such resurrection can redeem the horrors of all those who have "disappeared" in Argentina, in Guatemala, in China.

"In Christ all will be made alive" (1 Cor 15:22). For so many politically oppressed and devastated by continuing wars there is hope in imaging Christ as the first risen, in imaging others risen in his presence, and imaging an "end when Christ hands on the kingdom to God, when he will abolish all rule and all authority and power" (1 Cor 15:23-24). He rules until he puts all his enemies under his feet (1 Cor 15:25). "The last enemy death is abolished" (1 Cor 15:26).

Many in the first world can ignore death. Persons can be thirty years old and have never known someone who died and have never been to a funeral. The opposite is the situation with most women in the Third World. Death can be more dominant than life. Women can give birth to more children who die than who live. Even those who live beyond childhood may not live to the fullness of adulthood, much less to a long full life.

Although we may not relate to being baptized on behalf of dead persons (1 Cor 15:29), like Paula, women in the Third World "are in danger every hour." They "die daily" (1 Cor 15:30-31). With Paula they understand "fighting with wild beasts" (1 Cor 15:32). They have seen the sowing of seed that dies, but that then brings forth new life. Although the analogy limps, in the light of the glory of sun, moon, and stars, somehow the dead "sown in corruption is raised in incorruption" (1 Cor 15:42).

A cosmologist who each night wonders at the glory of the billions of stars can use language equally awe-inspiring: "Nothing is too wonderful to be true" (Herbert Friedman in *The Astronomer's Universe*, New York and London, 1990, xvi, quoting Michael Faraday).

Such is the mystery Paula has glimpsed:

> We shall all be changed,
>   in a moment,
>   in a glance of an eye . . . .

> Death will be swallowed up in victory . . .
>   but thanks to God
>   the one giving us the victory
>   through our Lord Jesus Christ.

> So, beloved sisters,
>   be firm, unmovable
>   abounding in the work of the Lord always,
>   knowing that your work
>   is not empty in the Lord (1 Cor 15:51-58).

1 Cor 16

Paula concludes her letter with concern for the needs in Jerusalem. She requests that each member of the assembly at Corinth on the first day of the week set aside an amount that can be gathered together when she comes. Some may go with her to take the gifts to Jerusalem (1 Cor 16:2-4). Paula recommends that they treat Timothea well if she comes for she "works the work of the Lord as I do" (1 Cor 16:10).

> Watch.
> Stand in the faith.
> Be a woman.
> Be strong.
> Let all your things be in Love (1 Cor 16:13-14).

Paula commends those who have helped her: Stephana, Fortunata, and Achaia. "They have refreshed my spirit and yours" (1 Cor 16:17-18). How often women of the Third World give thanks for the solidarity they find in one another. They find refreshment and strength in knowing they are not alone, that other women stand with them.

Paula sends greetings from the church of Asia (Asia Minor), especially from Aquila and Prisca and the church that is in their house (1 Cor 16:19). It is usually assumed that Aquila and Prisca are husband and wife. But may we also think of them as two women, not unlike the Mary and Martha of the gospel account? The gathering or assembly is in their house. They therefore preside and host the gatherings and meals which take place at their home.

> All the sisters greet you.
> Greet one another with a holy kiss (1 Cor 16:20).

Paula signs the letter, decries those who do not love the Lord, prays that the grace or gift of the Lord Jesus be with them and concludes: "My love be with you all in Christ Jesus" (1 Cor 16:24).

2 The Second Letter to the Corinthians:

Strength, Joy, and New Creation

Although most biblical scholars consider the Second Letter to the Corinthians a collection of several letters or fragments of letters, in this reflection we will study it as we have received it in the tradition. As we would expect, the introduction is parallel with that of the First Letter to the Corinthians. Paula names herself as apostle of Christ Jesus through the will of God and associates herself with Timothea writing to the gathering of God at Corinth and throughout the region of Achaia. She wishes them grace and peace from God our Father and the Lord Jesus Christ, whom she blesses as the Father of compassions and God of all strengthening. This God strengthens us in all our afflictions so that we may be able to strengthen others (2 Cor 1:1-4).

Not only that, but as the sufferings of Christ abound in us, so also the strengthening. Although this word for strengthening is a noun, its connotation both in classical Greek and in the New Testament easily slides over into the personal active dimension. It relates to invoking the gods as well as calling friends to be with one during a trial. The friends who do this become cheerleaders and support, those who cheer one on. The concept relates to the development of the Holy Spirit as comforter, as personal, as support.

Third World women understand the relationship between suffering and a deep strengthening, both of which can paradoxically come at the same time. And as Paula knew, this suffering/strengthening is also related to the suffering and strengthening of others. Such qualities give them hope that as they share in the struggle, so they share in the strengthening. Like Paula, they have suffered even to despair and the sentence of death. Their trust paradoxically is in the God who raises the dead, in the hope that he will deliver them. They trust not in a worldly wisdom but in the grace of God (2 Cor 1:5-12).

Like Paula these women work and travel against great odds, but with a singlemindedness that says: "Yes, God has anointed us, makes us strong in Christ and seals us with the Spirit in our hearts. We are co-workers with your joy" (2 Cor 1:22-24).

2 Cor 2, 3

These women come not to bring grief, but to bring joy. Because of the person of Christ, they forgive. In this way, they do not succumb to the temptations to vengeance characteristic of their antagonists. Satan, the adversary, can therefore have no advantage. On the contrary, God in Christ leads them to victory, out of life into life. They don't hawk the word of God, but with sincerity before God they speak in Christ (2 Cor 2:1-17).

These women do not commend themselves. They are the letter of Christ written by the Spirit of a living God, not on stone tablets but in their hearts. Their competence is not from themselves but from God who makes them competent as ministers of a new covenant, not in writing, but of the Spirit. The letter kills, but the Spirit makes alive. With such hope they are very bold, with their faces shining. The Lord is the Spirit, and where the Spirit of the Lord is, there is freedom (2 Cor 3:1-18).

2 Cor 4, 5

Like Paula, women of the Third World acknowledge their ministry. They are called to be open. They are called to proclaim not themselves, but Christ Jesus as leader of freedom, and themselves as facilitators to help bring about that freedom. The God who said, "Out of darkness light shall shine," shines in their hearts. Their enlightenment is in the knowledge of the glory of God which they see in the face of Jesus, and in the face of each woman, child, and man who reflect that face and who are entitled to the same dignity and respect they give to Jesus (2 Cor 4:1-6).

Like Paula, they recognize that this treasure is in earthenware vessels. What a contradiction—that treasure such as gold or jewels, rather than being placed in a guarded marble temple, is placed in jars made of clay, of the earth, easily breakable! Why should this be? So that the extravagance of the power may be of God and not of those women who are the ministers of that power (2 Cor 4:7).

How are the weaknesses manifested? Like Paula, these women are afflicted on every side, but not restrained; in difficulties, but not despairing; persecuted but not deserted; thrown down but not destroyed, always bearing about the dying of Jesus so that the life of Jesus in their bodies may be shown. From their dying comes life and freedom for those with whom they minister (2 Cor 4:8-12).

With Paula, these women have the same spirit of faith. They believe in human dignity and freedom; therefore they speak. The one who raised up Jesus will also present them to God. So they do not faint. Whatever their outward sufferings, their inward spirit is renewed day by day. The things seen are temporary; the things unseen are of the ages (2 Cor 4:13-18).

Even if the earthly house is destroyed, these women have a building of God, not made by hands, but of the ages. They walk through faith, not through appearance

(2 Cor 5:1-7). Whether they are considered sane or mad, it is the love of Christ that keeps them from falling apart. So in Christ there is a new creation. The old things are passing away; they are becoming new. All things are in God. God has reconciled all in Christ and given these women a ministry of reconciliation. So they are ambassadors for Christ, calling for dignity, respect, and human freedom (2 Cor 5:13-20).

2 Cor 6, 7

What is the work of ambassadors? They seize the time: "Now is an acceptable time. Now is the day of healing and wholeness" (2 Cor 6:2). Too long they have been told to wait, to not rock the boat. They have waited too long. They cannot wait any longer. While they strive not to offend, at the same time their ministry is from God. They endure much. They are beaten. They are in prison. At the same time, they strive for kindness, for a Holy Spirit, and for love that is real. They strive to speak in truth through the power of God. Their weapons are not guns, but justice. They are often dishonored. They are spoken ill of. They are dying, but at the same time they live. In spite of their grieving, they are always rejoicing. They are poor but enrich many. They have nothing, but they possess all things (2 Cor 6:4-10).

They are not to be yoked into compromise, whether it comes from military, political, or religious sources. Why should they succumb to the temples of consumerism, of oppressive power, of exploitation? They are a shrine of a living God for God says (2 Cor 6:14-16):

> I will dwell among them
> and I will walk among them,
> and I will be their God,
> and they shall be my people
> (2 Cor 6:16; Exod 25:8; 29:45).

Like Paula, these Third World women say: "Make room for us! We have wronged no one. We have injured no one. We have defrauded no one" (2 Cor 7:2). As Paul was strengthened by Titus, as Paula was strengthened by Tita, so these women are strengthened by their friends and by each other. When they hear good news from others or from other places, they rejoice that the God of freedom is moving (2 Cor 7:6).

2 Cor 8, 9

The Corinthians are rich in faith and word, in knowledge and diligence, and in love. They are generous with these gifts. Now they are asked to be generous out of their riches to those who are poor (2 Cor 8:7-8). It is perhaps ironic that the Third World women are those who for the most part have little of material wealth, but who are not only generous with whatever they have, but who ask on behalf of those in need, and who give of themselves—a sincerity of love that sometimes is rejected by those who have much, but which at the same time may inspire others to equal generosity. They know the gift of the Lord Jesus, that he became poor though he was rich so that through his poverty they might be rich (2 Cor 8:7-9). A person who sows seeds sparingly will harvest sparingly. A person who sows blessings will reap blessings (2 Cor 9:6).

2 Cor 10, 11

Paula sees her relationship with the Corinthians as paradoxical. Inspired by the gentleness of Christ, Paula sees herself as humble when she is with the Corinthians, but bold when she is away from them (2 Cor 10:1). But her letters are strong (2 Cor 10:11). Whatever the appearances or perceptions, one is not approved because she commends herself but because the Lord commends her (2 Cor 10:18).

The Jesus that is preached is a Jesus of simplicity (2 Cor 11:3-4). Paula knows her speech may be unskilled (2 Cor 11:6), but it is the truth of Christ that is in her (2 Cor 11:10).

Women theologians of the Third World can identify with many of the aspects Paula attributes to herself. They often are "humble" when with others. Like Paula's letters, their letters, speeches, or books are very strong. These women are not concerned with appearances, but leave any commendation to the Lord.

Some Third World women may see themselves as unskilled in speaking, but like Paula, their persuasiveness far outweighs any perceived inadequacies. Many of the women theologians have sharpened their speaking and writing skills through education and assiduousness, but there is a fire and a boldness that gives flame to the academic.

Paula is aware and the Third World women are aware that there are "false apostles, deceitful workmen" who call themselves "apostles of Christ. Even Satan can transform himself into an angel of light" (2 Cor 11:13-14).

Paula lists some qualities and events of her life with which Third World women can relate. Ironically comparing herself with some of the false apostles, Paula claims that she is Hebrew, she is an Israelite, she is the seed of Abraham. She is minister of Christ (2 Cor 11:22-23).

Third World women may be Mayan, Kenyan, Indian, but spiritually they are also Hebrew, Israelite, seed of Abraham and Sarah, and ministers of Christ. Again in irony and in comparing herself with false apostles, Paula boasts: "I have worked harder, I have been in prison more, I have been beaten more. I have died more" (2 Cor 11:23).

What gives fire to all of them is what they perceive as the truth of Christ and the truth of the justice that is demanded for women of the Third World.

Paula's account reads like a page from the account of some of the difficulties Rigoberta Menchû describes (Rigoberta Menchû, *I, Rigoberta Menchû: An Indian Woman in Guatemala*, edited and introduced by Elisabeth Burgos-Debray, London: Verso, 1984. Rigoberta received the Nobel Prize for Peace in 1992.) In fact,

Rigoberta's list in many ways is more shocking and exceeds the lists supplied by Paul:

> I was whipped thirty-nine times.
> Three times I was beaten with rods.
> Once I was stoned.
> Three times I was shipwrecked.
> I have been in the sea a night and a day.
> I have been in perils of rivers.
> I have been in perils from my own
> countrymen, from nations,
> perils in the city, in the wilderness,
>   in the sea, among false brethren,
> in work and hardship,
>   in watching many times,
> in famine and thirst,
>   in fasting many times,
> in cold and nakedness,
> conspirings against me daily,
> the care of the churches.
>
> Who is weak and I am not weak?
> Who is scandalized
>   and I am not on fire? (2 Cor 11:24-29).

2 Cor 12, 13

Unlike Paula, Third World women do not usually boast about any special visions or revelations they may have experienced. Even though Paula was no doubt speaking ironically, she nevertheless describes being "caught up into a third heaven" and not being sure whether this was an out-of-body experience (2 Cor 12:1-3). Third World women sense the Spirit is moving in powerful ways they do not understand, but the movement is in the concrete, in political and cultural cries for justice in the very earthy unjust situations they witness.

Yet, like Paula, they recognize their own weaknesses. They are most aware of their own limitations. Whatever Paula's "thorn in the flesh" was (2 Cor 12:7), Third World women know they have many "thorns in the flesh." With Paula they know that God's grace somehow is sufficient for them. God's power somehow is worked out though their weakness. So weaknesses, insults, persecutions, and difficulties on behalf of Christ and justice can somehow work the power of God (2 Cor 12:9). They are not working for personal gain; on the contrary, they are spending themselves (2 Cor 12:15) for building up the body of Christ. Such things as strife, jealousy, angers, rivalries, detraction, whispering, puffings up, disturbances (2 Cor 12:20) do not build justice, do not build the body of Christ.

Paula says she is coming to the Corinthians for a third time. Third World women like Rigoberta Menchû come again and again. Like Rigoberta, they may find themselves exiled from their own people. But they come again and again. They do not give up. Like Christ, who was crucified through weakness yet lives by the power of God, they are weak in Christ but they live by the power of God affecting people. So they ask others to examine themselves. Don't they perceive that Jesus Christ is in them unless they are counterfeits?

In conclusion, Paula expresses trust and urges that people act honestly (2 Cor 13:6-7). Somewhat surprisingly, she calls to them:

> Rejoice!
> Restore yourselves!
> Admonish yourselves!
> Think as one.
> Be at peace,
>   and the God of love and of peace
>   will be with you.
> Greet one another with a holy kiss.
> All the saints here send greetings.
>
> The grace of the Lord Jesus Christ
> and the love of God
> and the community of the Holy Spirit
> be with all of you (2 Cor 13:11-14).

Part Three:
Themes for Philemon,
Philippi, and Galatia

1 The Letter to Philemon:

Slavery, Freedom, and Relationships

The Letter to Philemon is unique among the original letters of Paul because it is written to an individual. Onesimus, a slave of Philemon, has run away and fled to Paula who is in prison, probably in Ephesus. She calls Philemon "dearly beloved and co-worker." The letter is from Paula and Timothea. Their letter is also addressed to "beloved Apphia" and Archippa, a co-worker, and the church in their house (Phlm 1:1-2).

Paula wishes them grace and peace from "God our Father and the Lord Jesus Christ." In the style of praise she learned as appropriate for a letter, Paula thanks God for Philemon and tells how she hears about Philemon's love and faith (Phlm 1:3-5). But she is working up to a special request. She even acknowledges how she is old and in prison, but nevertheless begs for her "child" Onesimus whom she "brought forth" in her bonds (Phlm 1:10).

Onesimus formerly was "useless" to his "owner" Philemon but now is "useful" both to Philemon and to Paula. Paula is sending Onesimus, a runaway slave, back to his owner Philemon and asks that he be received now not as a slave but beyond a slave, as a beloved brother. "If you think of me as sharing community with you, receive him as though you are receiving me" (Phlm 1:11-17).

Rather surprisingly, Paula then takes a practical approach. If Onesimus has wronged Philemon or owes anything, Paula says to put it on her account. She even signs her name as signature to pay, although she also notes how much Philemon owes to her. Paula knows Philemon will do more than Paula asks (Phlm 1:18-21).

Paula asks Philemon to prepare lodging because she hopes she will be able to come (Phlm 1:22). Paula adds that Epaphas, a co-prisoner in Christ Jesus, also sends greetings as do Mark, Aristarcha, Dema, and Luke, other co-workers. "The grace of the Lord Jesus Christ be with your spirit" (Phlm 1:23-25).

Are Third World women familiar with letters from prison? Yes: letters from their sisters and brothers, their mothers and fathers, letters they write to family, friends, and supporters, letters they write on behalf of others.

Letters from prison are a powerful genre. Too many people are in prison, and it seems as though even more persons will be in prison in the next century. The prisons are worldwide. Many persons are in prison for political reasons, some for no reason, some for speaking out for justice. Some like Onesimus are slaves. Amnesty International is one of the groups which work around the globe to free political prisoners.

Like Paula, anyone can write a letter on behalf of someone in prison. Third World women are working to free persons from the many kinds of slavery that still exist around the world.

2 The Letter to the Philippians:

Serving, Faith, and Rejoicing

Paula is in prison in Ephesus, a large beautiful city on the western edge of Asia Minor. She writes to the Philippians who are faithful to what they have learned previously when Paula was with them.

Paula and Timothea consider themselves servants of Jesus Christ (Phil 1:1). The word for servants is *douloi,* which is often translated as "slaves." Most modern readers hear this word as demeaning. In Scripture the word can be used this way, but it also can be used for that person closest to the sovereign. This person is so loyal that she or he will perform the lowliest service out of love. She identifies with the one she serves much as a loving wife or husband can speak for the one loved. In the ancient world, and still in some cultures today, the term refers to someone we think of more as a prime minister, one who is so identified with the one served that she can make treaties and speak for the one served.

Paula has found great strength and support from her good friend Timothea. Third World women have become newly conscious of the strength they find in each other as they share common goals.

In writing about "The Intifada, Nonviolence, and the Bible" (in *Feminist Theology from the Third World,* ed. by Ursula King, London and Maryknoll, N.Y.: SPCK/ Orbis Books, 1994), Jean Zaru, a Palestinian Christian, describes this new consciousness:

> As a Christian Palestinian woman, native of the Holy Land, I have been confronted all my life with social, economic, political, and religious structures of injustice that violated my dignity and self-esteem. The Church, as well as my mother, taught me not to resist, for this is not Christian. . . .
>
> The rebel in me started searching, agonizing, and asking questions. I kept asking myself, if we say there is something of God in every person, why is it often so difficult to see that presence of God in others? Why is there so much evil and suffering in the world? . . . I was happy to learn that the belief in the divinity seems to be part of all religions. "The kingdom of God is within you," said Jesus. "You are the temple of God," wrote Saint Paul. "He who knows himself knows God," said the Prophet Mohammed, and this is echoed by many Sufis. . . .
>
> In December 1987 our Intifada started. With it we created an atmosphere of nonviolent action—notice I say "action"—by which we hoped to resolve our problems of occupation and oppression and to promote peace. We started by affirming one another. All of us felt empowered. We had a sense of our own inner power and worth, young and old, men and women, rich and poor (230–231).

This sense of power and worth seems to be what Paula and Timothea found in each other and in the Philippians, "those saints in Christ Jesus with the bishops and deacons" (Phil 1:1). As Paula wishes them grace and peace, she thanks God with joy every time she remembers them in the community of the Good News from the first day until now. She is confident that the one who has begun a good work in them will complete it until the day of Christ Jesus. Paula prays that their love may more abound in full knowledge and in all perception (Phil 1:2-6, 9).

Paula sees that the events connected with her imprisonment have somehow advanced the Good News. Her bonds in Christ are evident to all in the praetorium and even to others. The other Christians have grown in confidence through Paula's bonds so that they dare to speak the Word of God. Some out of envy but others out of goodwill proclaim Christ. Whether through pretense or in truth, Christ is announced. Paula rejoices and will rejoice. The Spirit of Jesus will come through. Christ shall be magnified in her body, whether through life or through death. For to her to live is Christ and to die is gain (Phil 1:12-21).

With the Philippians, Paula will continue to move forward in the joy of the faith. She asks that they conduct themselves worthy of the Good News of Christ, that they stand in one spirit, that they not be terrified by their adversaries. Somehow it is given to them not only to believe in Christ but also to suffer on his behalf (Phil 1:25-29).

Phil 2

The theme of joy is strong in Paula's letters, but it is especially strong in the letter to the Philippians. It is a strong contrast to the fact that Paula is in prison and suffering in other ways. The paradox of life and death, of joy and suffering is one of the dominant insights which Paula understood from the death/resurrection of Christ.

Although suffering and death prevail for many Third World women, for some who are Christian there is a similar paradox of an experience of joy in their communion with each other, in their transcending love, and in an awareness that somehow their suffering is given meaning both by relationship of their common striving for justice, and by reason of their community in Christ. They can identify with Paula's words:

> If there is any strengthening in Christ,
> if any encouragement of love,
> if any community of spirit,

if any compassions and mercies,
fill up for me this joy
so that you think with one mind,
so that you have the same love,
are one in soul,
with your mind on one thing (Phil 2:1-2).

If they can work toward this unity, then Paula's warnings are appropriate corollary. They will not act out of rivalry nor pride. They will not think of themselves as better than others. They will look out for each other.

Paula incorporates in her letter a beautiful hymn that she may have modified, in which she encourages her readers to think as Christ who, although one with God, emptied himself, taking the form of a slave *(doulou)*, became human, and was obedient unto death, death on a cross. It is for this reason that God has lifted him up and given him a name above every name so that in that name everyone should acknowledge that the Lord Jesus Christ is to the glory of God the Father (Phil 2:5-11).

Third World women know this emptying even to death, and they trust that somehow with Christ their emptying will simultaneously be an exaltation, a lifting up, a resurrection. It is God who works through them. They do all things without murmurings or disputes. They are blameless and harmless in the midst of a perverted and crooked generation. They shine as lights in the world. They hold forth the word of life. They rejoice even if they are offered as sacrifice for the cause of justice (Phil 2:13-17).

Paula sends Timothea and Epaphrodita, who has been sick, as her companions in labor both to be strengthened and to strengthen. Joy and gladness go with them all (Phil 2:19, 25-29).

Phil 3

In spite of all the difficulties, Paula again tells the Philippians to rejoice in the Lord (Phil 3:1). Nevertheless, they should beware of evil workers and of those who "cut" (Phil 3:2). "We worship God in the Spirit and we rejoice in Christ Jesus" (Phil 3:3). "The things I used to count as worth having, I now count as worthless because of my commitment to Christ" (Phil 3:7).

It is through her faith in Christ that she knows Christ and the power of the resurrection, but this resurrection includes communion with the sufferings of Christ and being conformed to Christ's death. As Christ laid hold of Paula, so Paula hopes to lay hold of Christ. She forgets those things which lie behind and stretches forward to the future. Her conversation is in heaven (Phil 3:9-13, 20).

This combination of suffering and resurrection is what the Third World women know so intimately. Yet somehow they also know joy. The things they valued before their call to justice are no longer their prime values. Like Paula they stretch toward the future.

Phil 4

The last section addressed to the Philippians is a crescendo of exaltation and rejoicing. Paula rejoices in those she calls her dearly beloved, the ones she longs for, her joy and her crown. She calls them as beloved to stand in the Lord (Phil 4:1). She begs Euodia and Syntyche to think as one in the Lord. She asks the one with whom she has been "yoked" to help those other women who have struggled with her and also with Clementia and the other co-workers whose names are in the book of life (Phil 4:2-3).

> Rejoice in the Lord always!
> Again I say rejoice! (Phil 4:4).

"The Lord is near . . . Don't worry about anything. Use prayer, petitions, and giving thanks to let God know your requests and the peace of God which exceeds all understanding will guard your hearts and thoughts in Christ Jesus" (Phil 4:5-7).

All these words are ones Third World women can relate to. Friendships and interrelationships are crucial to those working for justice. Bonding is strengthened to the point of transcending suffering and calling each other to rejoice. Prayer is often basic and in a violent situation peace can sometimes prevail.

Paula loves lists. She no doubt learned many of them as she was growing up since such lists were common in the Mediterranean educational world. She also seems talented in modifying the lists to suit her Christian communities. A universality comes out in some of these directives which gives great hope for a new millennium and a new global community. Such a community is not bound by narrow sectarian prejudices. "Whatsoever things are true, honest, just, pure, lovable, well-spoken of—think about these things, which you have learned and received . . . and the God of peace will be with you" (Phil 4:8-9).

Like Paula, Third World women know how to be humbled, how to abound when largess comes, how to be full and how to be hungry. They can do all things through Christ who strengthens them (Phil 4:12-13). Paula prays that the grace of our Lord Jesus Christ will be with them (Phil 4:23).

3 The Letter to the Galatians:

Evils, Faithfulness, and the Christ Who Dwells Within

Paula's Letter to the Galatians is known as the Good News of Christian freedom. It begins with a typical address and prayer of praise.

Gal 1–2

Paula is an apostle, one who is sent, but sent "not from men or through men, but through Jesus Christ and God the Father, the one who raised Christ from the dead" (Gal 1:1). Paula joins with all her sisters to greet those gathered in the churches in Galatia (central Asia Minor). To them she sends grace and peace from God our Father and the Father of Jesus Christ. This Jesus is the one who gave himself for our sins so as to lift us out of this present evil age according to God's will. To him is glory to the ages of the ages. So be it.

Is this present age evil? Persons in developed nations would rather not think so, but an honest look at newspapers and even personal experience reveal problems that are rightly named evil: sicknesses with pain and no cure; oppression or dysfunction in relationships; murders, especially of the innocent.

Drive-by murders are becoming commonplace in some cities in the United States. Bombs which kill many innocent persons are no longer confined to perceived "terrorist" locations. Children and others are homeless through no fault of their own. Even a suburban school can have twenty-five or thirty homeless children for whom teachers will start an after-school program because the children have nowhere to go. Children are scavengers in the garbage heaps of Mexico City and in other cities as a means of survival.

There are many non-evil and beautiful aspects of our age. Perhaps they are even more dominant than the evil aspects, but the evils are so horrendous that they certainly characterize many parts of our age. Certainly in some parts of the world at some times there is no question of an apparent dominance of evil.

No wonder, then, that persons can look to a God who will lift them out of these evils. What is the Good News which Paula sees as lifting her out of these evils? It is that tradition of death-resurrection in Christ to which she has been faithful over many years.

How many women today have a tradition and history of faithfulness, even much longer than that of Paula! Sometimes, even though they were abused as children, they have survived and healed and spent a lifetime of loving and faithfulness even into their nineties. Like Paula confronting Peter to his face over matters of injustice (Gal 2:11), they have often been surprised to find themselves confronting others, even authorities, on matters of injustice. Perhaps it is, for example, Rigoberta Manchû who is surprised to find herself a leader for justice in Guatemala—speaking out, confronting authorities, being faithful to a tradition of life-death-resurrection.

How well these women may say with Paula:

For I through law
  died to the law
so that I might live to God.

With Christ I have been co-crucified
    and I live, no more I,
but Christ lives in me,
and what I now live in the flesh,
by faith I live in the Son of God who loves me
    and gives himself up for me (Gal 2:19-20).

Gal 3–6

Women of the Third World today may well say to some who call themselves Christians, "O foolish Christians, who has bewitched you? Before your eyes Jesus Christ has been portrayed as crucified" (Gal 3:1).

When Archbishop Romero started talking with the poor, he realized that many of the laws, and even what was interpreted as *the* Law, whether civil or church, no longer brought the Spirit. The Spirit would have to come by faith (Gal 3:2). The work of faith led him to become an advocate for the poor and the embodiment of Christ crucified and risen. So many Christians begin "in the Spirit" but succumb to "the flesh" (Gal 3:3). Christ brings a new covenant, a new law of faith and the Spirit. We are all children of God not because we are heirs of Abraham and Sarah, not because we keep the "Law" or certain laws, but because of "faith in Christ Jesus" (Gal 3:26).

There is a new transformation. Those who are baptized in Christ have died with him and rise with him. They "put on Christ" (Gal 3:27). Since all are Christ, class distinctions and hierarchies no longer exist. We no longer distinguish Jews from non-Jews. We no longer discriminate those called slaves from those called free. We no longer make hierarchy according to gender. "There is no longer male and female for you are all one in Christ Jesus" (Gal 3:28).

Women are no longer under "tutors and governors," no longer slaves, no longer in bondage, because in the fullness of time God sent forth her Child, grown from a woman so that those who were under the Law are now made children of God. And because we are children,

God has sent the spirit of her Child into our hearts. We are heirs of God (Gal 4:2-7).

There are those who choose to remain in bondage, but women theologians of the Third World are choosing to take God seriously. They are choosing to be free in Christ. Paula says to such women:

> Christ freed us.
> Therefore stand firm.
> Don't get entangled again
>   with a yoke of slavery (Gal 5:1).

But women so freed are not to use this freedom for selfish reasons. Indeed they are called to serve one another (Gal 5:13). The "Law" is fulfilled in the saying: "Love your neighbor as yourself" (Gal 5:14). Be careful not to "bite and devour" one another or you may destroy one another (Gal 5:15). If you are led by the Spirit, you are not under the "Law." What is the fruit of the Spirit?—not fornication, jealousy, drunken revelings (Gal 5:18-19), but:

> Love, joy, peace,
> endurance, kindness, goodness,
> faithfulness, meekness, self-control (Gal 5:22).

Those who belong to Christ have crucified their lusts and passions that enslave. Paula says: "If we live in the Spirit, let us also walk in the Spirit" (Gal 5:24-25).

We are to bear one another's burdens. That is how we fulfill the law of Christ (Gal 6:2). "Bearing one another's burdens" takes on new meaning for women theologians who return to Korea and are overwhelmed by feelings of solidarity with persecuted poor women. A similar tension also exists for African women theologians who recognize that Christianity has often meant not freedom but oppression such as abuse or being economically abandoned.

It is difficult not to lose heart (Gal 6:8). They know they are being crucified with Christ (Gal 6:14), but such death can lead to a "new creation" (Gal 6:15).

Paula wishes them peace and mercy. Like Christ, Paula bears in her body the stigmata, the marks of the wounds of Christ (Gal 6:16-17). So also do many of these Third World women whose bodies hang on the crosses of famine, prostitution, dislocation, and poverty. They cry out for freedom.

Part Four:
Major Theological
Development for Rome

1 The Letter to the Romans:

Giftedness and Universality

Paula's Letter to the Romans, perhaps written from Corinth, is thought by many to be Paula's most important letter. Especially treasured in the Protestant tradition, it seems to be more than a letter since it includes much developed theological thought.

It is not clear how the Christian group began in Rome, but since there was already an established group of Jews, it may have begun from that center. At any rate, by the time of Paula's writing, there is an important community of Christians at Rome.

Rom 1

In her address, Paula calls herself once again "a servant of Jesus Christ, called to be an apostle" (Rom 1:1). She understands herself as "separated" for the Good News, for the gospel of God.

Using a tradition which she reflects from the communities and to which she also contributes, Paula recalls the work of God and her people. As recorded in the Holy Writings, God promised through the prophets that the son from the seed of David and Bathsheba is designated Son of God in power according to the Spirit of holiness by a resurrection of the dead (Rom 1:2-4).

It is through Jesus that Paula received grace and her call to be an apostle among all the nations. But those to whom she writes are also called, all those in Rome who are beloved of God. She wishes them grace and peace from God Father of us and of the Lord Jesus Christ for the faith of the Romans being announced "in all the world" (Rom 1:8). Since it is a faith she shares with them, she hopes to come to be with them. Just as she owes much to Greeks and foreigners, to the wise and those without knowledge, so she hopes to come to bring the Good News to the Romans. Far from being ashamed of this Good News, she knows it is the power of God for wholeness for everyone with faith, to Jew, to Greek, to those with faith. "For the just will live by faith" (Rom 1:12-17).

Like Paula, women theologians of the Third World are reaching out in a solidarity that sometimes surprises them. Korean women theologians recognize that despite cultural differences, they are involved in a development which parallels that of Indian women theologians or Philippine women theologians. As they have met at regional conferences, they have recognized a kinship. Like Paula, they write to each other, and read each other's theological insights. They are strengthened by each other's faith. They hope to visit each other.

In Romans 1:18-32, Paula describes the view which many Jews and Christians of the first century evidently used to interpret the corruption which seemed to dominate their society. The impiety and unrighteousness they see as calling forth the wrath of God.

To them the invisible things of God are clearly seen from the material things they see around them. People knew God but because of their vanity their hearts were darkened. They asserted themselves to be wise but became foolish. They changed the glory of the incorruptible God into the images of human beings, of birds, of animals and reptiles.

The remains of such images are seen all around the Mediterranean, hundreds of statues, sometimes half-animal half-human god-figures, and reptiles. To walk among the excavations or to observe in the museums in Greece or Turkey is to be overwhelmed as the Jews and Christians of the first century were.

Such images were interrelated with the political, religious, economic, and social structures of the cultures. The first-century Jews and Christians saw the immorality of the times as a result of such idolatry. They called the desires of hearts uncleanness. They saw persons as dishonoring their bodies among themselves, serving the creature more than the creator. They were aware, for example, of the brothels near the temples, of temple prostitution, of the cultural "convenience" and exploitation of young men often by older men. Such activities were abhorrent to Jews and Christians.

The lists reflect the stories in the newspapers of today: wickedness, covetousness, evil, envy, murder, strife, malignity; persons who are rumormongerers, backbiters, haters of God, insolent, arrogant, boasters, inventors of evil things, disobedient to parents, undiscerning, faithless, without natural affection, unmerciful (Rom 1:29-31).

The consciousness raising of Third World women theologians has brought them to an acknowledgment of similar immoralities today in all our societies. The response at first is one of shock: such things cannot be. But naming the evils is a step toward the truth. The evils can no longer be ignored.

Rom 2

But Paula then turns the tables, in a style not unlike that of the Hebrew prophets such as Amos. You are inexcusable if you so judge. You condemn yourself because you are doing the same things (Rom 2:1). The division is that between those who endure, who work good, seeking glory, honor, incorruption, and the life of the ages, as contrasted with those who are self-seeking, disobeying the truth, and succumbing to wrath and anger (Rom 2:7-8).

Paula was constantly pointing out the value and the misuse of the law, whether it was the Jewish law for Jews, civil laws for citizens, or the law of God written in the hearts of persons. Unfortunately, we have similar problems of misuse of the law today, especially among peoples of the Third World or people of minority groups.

Government sources in the United States indicate that Black Americans are far from being the highest number of users of drugs in the United States. At the same time, Black Americans number a very high percentage of those who are imprisoned for drug-related incidents. In many parts of the Third World, the "law" is used to quell the cries of those crying out for justice. Such persons are imprisoned, "disappear," are tortured or killed, are exiled, often under the aegis of the "law." Aquinas notes that a "law" that is unjust is not a law, yet human beings have a way of using "law" for their own purposes.

Third World women theologians have become conscious of how incongruous the judgments of the "law" or of authorities administering the "law" often are when it comes to the injustices imposed on the poor, especially on women. Throughout the world, women prostitutes are arrested, fined, or scorned, while their men customers usually go untouched. Women who are raped are told to keep quiet, and find the "law" very difficult to use for their defense, while those who rape usually go untouched. The contrasts of the use and misuse of "law" are contemporary problems throughout all societies.

Third World women may well say to their oppressors:

> You have persuaded yourself
> that you are a guide of the blind,
> a light in darkness,
> an instructor of the foolish,
> a teacher of infants,
> having the form of knowledge,
> and of the truth in the law.

But if you are teaching others,
why don't you teach yourselves?
You proclaim that one should not steal
but aren't you stealing?

You say not to commit adultery,
but don't you commit adultery?
You say you detest idols,
but don't you rob temples?

If the work is of the heart
and the spirit,
then praise is not from men
but from God (Rom 2:19-22, 29).

Rom 3

As Paul and Paula wrestled especially with the Jewish law of their time, so Third World women wrestle with the contradictions between "law" and justice in their times. Like Paula, they strive not to succumb to a false righteousness. Quoting the Psalms and Isaiah, with Paula they can say:

There is not a righteous person,
no, not one;
there is not one understanding,
there is not one seeking God.
All are turned away,
together become unprofitable.
There is not one doing kindness,
no, not so much as one.

Their throat is like an open grave.
With their tongues they act deceitfully.
The poison of asps is under their lips.
Their mouth is full of cursing and bitterness.

Their feet are swift to shed blood.
Ruin and misery are their ways.
A way of peace they do not know.
There is no fear of God
    before their eyes (Rom 3:10-18).

What can we say of the exploitation by so-called developed nations and worldwide corporations who often in the name of profits ignore the "law," make their own "laws," and interpret the "laws" for their profits? Third World women theologians have hardly begun to see the evils at this level. They see the levels of corruption close at hand. Like Paula, they name the evils they are witnessing. They call for justice. They are speaking out on behalf of those they identify with.

But where are the prophets who can address the national, international, corporate, and global challenges? There are some. There is Jim Wallis who continues a worldwide political stance in the hope of building peace and justice. There are those national leaders who often jeopardize their own political futures and who sometimes are assassinated for their stands. There are those corporate leaders who speak out, who act and who often lose their positions, whether it be in tobacco-related industries; agricultural one-crop exploitation; bottling industries; clothing, shoe, and textile worker oppression; arms sales. There are investors who take a stand as stockholders to resist exploitation. They are the ones who listen to the cries from the Third World women. Action is called for from all levels.

All come short. It is God's grace that brings justice. It is Christ who pays the price for the sinfulness and injustice throughout the world. He is the one who compensates through faith. The law is the law of faith (Rom 3:23-27). The idea of an eye for an eye, of retaliation no longer holds. All are responsible, in one way or another. We are all part of a whole, part of the brokenness and part of the healing.

Just as Paul and Paula found heroes of faith in Abraham and Sarah, so Third World women theologians find heroes of faith and justice in Jesus and Mary, often in their parents and grandparents, but especially in others who are speaking out or acting out their convictions. Rigoberta Menchû testifies to these influences in her book *I, Rigoberta Menchû*. María Pilar Aquino in her book *Our Cry for Life* quotes Argentine writer Beatríz Melano-Couch:

> The news of the reign of God shows me that I am created by God to be free and also to be the author of my own destiny in his sight, not a slave to other human beings. . . . The news of God's reign tells me that I am destined for God, not for torture, or the death penalty, but for freedom, peace, joy, and fulfillment (Beatríz Melano-Couch, "El Reino de Dios y la ética," in Ivone Gebara et al., *Apuntes y aportes de la mujer ecuménica*, Cuaderno Pastoral 5 [APE-FEC, Mendoza, Argentina, 1987] 104, quoted by Aquino on 190).

Rom 4

"Beyond hope they believe in hope" (Rom 4:18).

For some, this faith and hope lead them beyond what they have known of an oppressive Western Christianity. Chung Kyung, for example, writes, "I do not know what kind of new spirituality and theology will come out of Asian women's struggle to be authentically who we are in the fullest sense. I do know, however, that the future of Asian women's spirituality and theology must move away from Christo-centrism and toward life-centrism" (*Struggle To Be the Sun Again*, 114). Others, however, like Paula, still find a cry for freedom in placing faith in one who has raised Jesus our Lord out of the dead (Rom 4:24).

Rom 5

This faith makes justice, so there is peace with God through our Lord Jesus Christ. With Paula, Third World women theologians stand and rejoice in hope of the glory of God (Rom 5:2), but the glory of God is human being fully alive. Like Paula, they even boast of their afflictions because their sufferings work patience, patience offers proof, and proof offers hope. Such hope does not put them to shame because the love of God has been poured out in their hearts through the Holy Spirit given to them (Rom 5:3-5).

Paula then develops the idea that Christ died for the ungodly. The contrast is sharp: one will hardly die for a just person. Nevertheless, because of God's love for us, while we are sinners, Christ died for us. We are made just by his blood (Rom 5:6-9).

These are images close to the experience of many Third World women. Aquino quotes Ignacio Ellacuría:

> The fundamental principle on which the new order is based is that all should have life and have it more abundantly (Jn 10:10). The historical experience of death, either through want and hunger or through repression, or through different kinds of violence, an experience that is so common in Latin America, shows the fundamental importance of material life as the first gift from which all else follows. This life must be filled out by inner growth and in relation to others always in search of more life and a better life ("Diez Afirmaciones sobre Utopía y Profetismo desde América Latina," *Sal Terrae*, 12 [1988] 889, quoted by Aquino on 190).

It is striking that Aquino adds to a footnote (!) that "Ellacuría bore witness to this conviction by his death" (235).

But even those who do not die shed their blood. Kyung quotes a poem by one of these women, Gabriele Dietrich, of German origin, who has worked in South India since 1972, and who identifies and works with Indian women in the movement.

I am a woman
and my blood
cries out:

Who are you
to deny life
to the life-givers?

    ***

But i(sic) have learned
to love my sisters.
We have learned
to love one another.
We have learned
even to respect
ourselves.

I am a woman
and my blood
cries out (Kyung, 66–67, 70).

The hope of Paula and of other Christians, as well as of those who continue to strive for good in spite of the evils they confront, somehow transcends the evil. For Christians, the gift in Christ is more abundant than the evil. Grace not only overcomes sin, but thrusts itself into the life of the ages "through Jesus Christ our Lord" (Rom 5:17, 20-21).

Rom 6

For Paula, as sin and grace are parallel, so are death to sin and life through grace. Such death and life come through death and burial with Christ through baptism, and being raised up to walk in newness of life (Rom 6:3-4). "For if we grow together in the likeness of his death, we shall also be in the likeness of his resurrection" (Rom 6:5). Paula then says it another way: "Our old being was crucified with him so that the body of sin might be destroyed . . . One who is dead is cleared of sin. If we died with Christ, we believe that we shall also live with him. We know that Christ raised from the dead dies no more. Death is lord of him no more" (Rom 6:6-9).

This experience of going through death is common to women of the Third World. Many girl children are not even allowed to be born, or are cast off soon after they are born. The percentage of males in China now outdistances the percentage of females. The statistical difference is large enough to suggest that an abnormal number of female child deaths is responsible. How this affects not only individuals and families, but also the future of the genetic code and society is open to speculation.

The kind of death Paula is speaking of is once. Like Christ, she and women of the Third World experience a death to an old way of life. They turn from that and, whatever their weaknesses, they live thrust toward God. They are alive through Christ (Rom 6:10-11). They are free (Rom 6:18). This is the gift of the life of the ages through Christ (Rom 6:23).

Rom 7

In the context of the law of the times, Paula uses the analogy of a woman bound by law to her husband while he is alive (Rom 7:1-3). This context is true not only of women two thousand years ago. It is true of most women today as we enter into the twenty-first century.

Paula experiences great freedom in her sense of being "delivered from the law" which she found oppressive. This freedom leads to serving others in the "newness of the Spirit" (Rom 7:6). Like Paula and the early Christians, Third World women often feel oppressed by the laws and the interpretation of those laws. Many try to work within those laws, but find a contradiction between the laws as carried out and the call to freedom which they find in the stories from the Scriptures.

Whether the stories are about Moses and Miriam or Jesus and Mary, the women are inspired by the respect for individuals, by the recognition that laws or misinterpreted laws from the pharaoh or from civil or religious authorities need to be resisted, that a call to freedom is often countercultural, and may even lead to rejection, suffering, and death. Laws can be "holy and good" (Rom 7:12), but misused they can "produce death" (Rom 7:13).

Paula recognizes the contradiction within herself, that sometimes she wills to do an action but does not follow through with practice, that sometimes she even does what she hates (Rom 7:15).

Third World women also know their own weaknesses and contradictions, but many would reject Paula's statement that nothing good dwells in her or in her flesh (Rom 7:18).

On the contrary, many women are only now coming to acknowledge the goodness of their own bodies, the goodness of the natural functions of their flesh. For too long, Paul's or Paula's recognition of weakness and even inclination to sin have been applied to all functions of the body and thereby for two thousand years have been used as concepts to oppress especially women, to destroy their sense of being temples of the Spirit, of being made in the image of God.

Third World women are on the edge of a major revolution to reject such oppression and to find in religious or other images a sense of dignity, of respect, of human rights to autonomy and freedom. Some Third World women theologians are providing leadership as they struggle with their own consciousness-raising, their own religious or political controversies. Some find courage in Jesus as a leader toward freedom.

Rom 8

The law was not adequate for Paula and the early Christians (Rom 8:3). It is not adequate for women today. They find a new "law of the Spirit of life in Christ Jesus" which makes them free (Rom 8:2). Somehow this takes place through Jesus who by becoming fully human was able to transform the weaknesses of flesh into a full human life in the Spirit (Rom 8:3-5). If one has the "Spirit of Christ," "the Spirit of God dwells in you" (Rom 8:9). "The Spirit of the one who raised Jesus from the dead" also "dwells in you" and gives you life (Rom 8:11). Therefore, you are adult children of God (Rom 8:16). As children you are "heirs of God and joint heirs with Christ" (Rom 8:17).

Third World women believe that the "sufferings of this life are not worthy to be compared with the glory" to come (Rom 8:18). Creation is groaning, waiting eagerly for deliverance from bondage into freedom (Rom 8:19-23). Third World women are groaning and crying out, are working and struggling for the freedom which is their right in the ongoing creation.

That is why their hope is so inspiring. They do not see what they hope for, but they hope for what they do not see. They wait for it eagerly (Rom 8:24-25). It is the Spirit who groans within and prays for a new world which is coming (Rom 8:26). For many women of the Third World this is a political groaning where the spiritual is not separated from the political or religious. It is one human struggle.

Paula writes: "The sufferings of this present time cannot be compared with the glory which will be revealed in us" (Rom 8:18). For two thousand years this concept has often been used to oppress people in their sufferings, to condone their sufferings in exchange for the promise of "pie in the sky." Unfortunately, the concept is still widely used today, so much so that, not only Third World women, but even women in the so-called developed nations often put up with persecution, rape, battering, unjust wages because their families, their societies, their cultures have inculcated their sense of themselves as sufferers in their present lives, with a vague promise that things will get better or that they deserve to suffer, that they are punished for their presumed wrongdoing. This understanding is contradicted by the context of this saying, as well as by the major thrust of Paula's letters, and by the call to freedom in Christ.

Though a human being may suffer, the call is to new life and resurrection. Though a person suffers injustice, the call is to strive for justice. Though one experiences unfreedom, the call is to cry for freedom. No one is called to be victim, but to struggle for and claim transformation.

On the other hand, Paula recognizes, and so do women of the Third World, that at present the mystery of suffering is part of the human condition for most persons. Psychologists even show that persons acknowledged as leaders, or wisdom figures, always count suffering as part of their growth. But Third World women theologians are recognizing that suffering as evil must not be attributed to the will of God. Suffering in itself is not good, although persons can bring good out of suffering.

For Christians suffering is always seen as associated with the suffering of Christ. Suffering is at least given a language and an image, the suffering Christ, whose pain somehow brings resurrection or new life, and whose suffering gives a cosmic dimension to the brokenness of human life. It is even the experience of some that suffering can be redemptive; it can somehow be linked to freedom for the self and others, to reconciliation and new life.

Somehow the brokenness of creation becomes part of the freedom of God's children. There is a Spirit that sometimes helps persons in their weakness (Rom 8:26), a Spirit that is bigger than the universe. Somehow there is design in the universe, although for the most part we know only the design of chaos.

Paula raises another difficult problem in saying that for those who love God all things work together for good (Rom 8:28). The victims of the holocaust, as well as other victims through time, whether in Armenia, Bosnia, China, Africa, or Guatemala, certainly make this saying seem simplistic. But there are persons like Bonhoeffer, Corrie Ten Boom, Anne Frank, Viktor Frankl, who survive and transcend evil, and who refuse to submit to despair. Many Third World women experience comparable evils and they too refuse to despair.

It is a strange phenomenon of psychology that those who believe in the possibility of good often contribute to the coming of the good, whether it be healing or achievement that is involved. Some traditions call this a destiny prearranged (Rom 8:30). Others find a narrow interpretation too elitist and too simplistic. There are too many variables to easily name a destiny. "If God is for us, who can be against us?" (Rom 8:31) too often has been and is the cry of the oppressive conqueror.

Can Third World women relate to such a saying? Most have heard the words on the lips of the oppressor, whether misused civil authority or misused church authority. But there are some who identify God with the call to freedom and recognize the hypocrisy and distortion of such a phrase used against justice. With Paula, they acknowledge the mystery that God "did not spare her own Son" (Rom 8:32) and daughters.

Tribulation, persecution, famine do not necessarily separate women from the love of Christ. They know famine, nakedness (Rom 8:35), torture, and guns. They are "killed all day long. They are thought of as sheep for the slaughter" (Rom 8:36). Neither death nor life separates them from the love of God (Rom 8:38-39).

Rom 9

When Paula says that her grief is a great and incessant pain in her heart (Rom 9:2), Third World women can relate. Paula's conflict is between those who seemed to be favored by God, and those who have received God's mercy. In religious terms, the "establishment" Israel has everything: covenants, law, promises (Rom 9:4). Their leaders, Abraham, Sarah, Isaac, Jacob, Moses, Miriam, were "chosen." Nevertheless, too many of the people have not been true.

Paula quotes the prophet Hosea: "I will call those not-my-people my-people, and the not-loved those who are loved" (Rom 9:25; Hos 2:23). In the same place (Hos 1:10) where it was said, "You were not my people," they will be called "children of a living God" (Rom 9:25-26).

Poor people of Guatemala, poor people of South Africa experienced being "not-loved," and moreover were treated as slaves, were imprisoned, tortured, and killed. Yet, now, some trickle of mercy has reached them.

Using another image, Paula quotes Isaiah that "the remnant will be saved" (Rom 9:27). Some Third World Christians see themselves as the remnant, the poor who have remained faithful. Somehow God is with them. Through struggle, the blood of martyrs, elections hard won, and courageous leaders, justice seems possible.

Rom 10

Just as early Christians had difficulty with the false righteousness of some zealots (Rom 10:2), so Third World women theologians have difficulty with those who pride themselves as favored by God or as keepers of the law, while at the same time they are blind to oppression and the needs of justice. To affirm the *status quo* as the will of God, to deny the rights of the poor, to hide behind the injustices of the falsely rich and powerful is to not believe in Jesus—Jesus who died but who came to life (Rom 10:9). A good heart leads to faith (Rom 10:10).

> For there is no difference
> of Jew and Greek.
> The same Lord of all
> is rich to all who call on him (Rom 10:12).

Third World women might say:

> For there is no difference
> of rich and poor.
> The same Lord of all
> is rich to all who call on him.

But how will the falsely righteous believe the equality of rich and poor in Jesus if they haven't heard about it? (Rom 10:14). "And how will they hear about it unless there is preaching? And how will they preach if they are not sent? How beautiful those announcing good things!"

(Rom 10:15). "Faith comes from hearing and hearing through the Word of Christ" (Rom 10:17). Third World women know that they must preach the truth about injustice. They must herald the call to justice. They must speak out as Jesus spoke out, whatever the consequences.

Rom 11

Does God reject the rich and powerful, the "establishment"? (Rom 11:1). No. But although the powerful kill prophets (Rom 11:3), nevertheless, there will be left a remnant (Rom 11:5). The conversion comes by grace, not by works. Bishop Romero listened to the poor, and grace came, grace to acknowledge the injustices from those in power, grace to speak out for the poor. Like other prophets, including Elias, he was left to stand alone (Rom 11:3). And like other prophets, he was killed. However, those in El Salvador experience his continuing presence.

What is this mystery of grace, that some accept the gift, yet others are in torpor? They have "eyes not to see and ears not to hear" (Rom 11:8).

Third World women do not seek vengeance. They hope for the conversion of their oppressors. In fact, if the oppressors should be converted to justice, the Third World women will rejoice. Like a fruitful olive tree, some come to justice by nature. Others are grafted in (Rom 11:24). Whatever the process, Third World women hope for conversion of oppressors and oppressed. All are dependent on God's mercy (Rom 11:32).

O the depth of riches, wisdom,
    and knowledge of God.
How inscrutable God's judgments
    and how unsearchable her ways.
Who has first known the mind of the Lord?
    Or who is the Lord's counselor?

Or who previously gave to God
and God will repay her?
Because of God and through God
and to God are all things.
To God be glory to the ages (Rom 11:33-36).

Rom 12

Women of the Third World can relate to Paula's summary admonition: "Don't be conquered by the evil, but conquer the evil by the good" (Rom 12:21).

Paula had learned well the practical philosophies which were part of common culture in the Mediterranean world. Like others, she learned lists of desired behaviors and attitudes. Through sanctions and codes, she had learned what were accepted ways of acting. Chapter 12 in Romans is largely an exhortation to such actions, but placed in the context of Christians surrounded by a culture sometimes inimical to such values.

The first exhortation is one which women would at first sight reject, and one which unfortunately has often been used to subject women to oppressions of various kinds. What was the cultural context then, and what is it now? Although Paula stands at the cross, such a stance is always directed to life, in fact, the fullness of life. So "life" may be a key to the exhortation:

I beseech you
through compassion of God,
present your bodies
a living, holy sacrifice,
well pleasing to God,
your reasonable service (Rom 12:1).

Women's bodies are not to be sacrificed in the Roman or Greek temples. They are not to be sacrificed by prostitution or slavery. They are living and holy, created by God, and, therefore, well pleasing to God. Their use of their bodies is to be reasonable and as liturgy or worship of God.

An older formula in marriage included the expression: "With my body I worship you." This was seen as the deepest form of mutual love. So Paula is calling the early Christians to value their bodies, to see them as called to the use of reason and logic and indeed worship of God. Concomitantly, they are not to go along with the age they are living in, but they are to be transformed by renewing their minds which will show the will of God as good, pleasing, and directed toward the future.

What does this mean for Third World women? They need to reject servitude. They need to claim the dignity of their bodies. They need to renew their minds so they can be transformed themselves and thereby also transform the age for themselves, for their children, and for the societies of which they are part.

Some women from developing nations, reflecting on the story of the Canaanite woman (Matt 15:21-28), spell out the implications in forceful language:

(1) As leaders, facilitators, catalysts, animators in development, we have nothing to lose as we challenge superiors, people in authority and power structures that hold us in bondage. The woman in the story demonstrates through her selfless courage that she had nothing to lose and everything to gain if she could only get Jesus' attention and his help in healing her daughter.

(2) Women need to be aware of their strengths and use them to their advantage. The Canaanite woman knew she was good with words and turned her strength into an advantage when she debated with Jesus.

(3) Women need to be able to handle conflict and not run away from situations that seem oppressive. They need to develop the skills to stand up to men when they use masculinity as a form of oppression.

(4) Through standing firm in the face of discrimination, women can educate men and force them into making choices. By challenging Jesus to recognize her need, the woman learned that Jesus' message was to non-Jews as well as to the Jews (King, *op. cit.*, 203–204).

This is not to oppress others but to recognize that the members of a body have different actions, all working together. Many persons are one body in Christ, members of one another and of the one body (Rom 12:4-5). The gifts differ. Some prophesy according to faith. Some minister. Some teach. Some exhort. Some share with simplicity. Some lead with responsibility. Some show mercy with cheerfulness (Rom 12:6-8). With Paula, Third World women can say:

Let love be unassuming.
Shrink from evil.
Cleave to the good.

Love each other warmly.
Let the spirit burn.

Rejoice in hope.
Endure affliction.
Be steadfast in prayer.

Give to the needs of all.
Pursue hospitality.

If people persecute you,
bless them.
Do not curse.

Rejoice with those who rejoice.
Weep with those who weep.

Seek peace.

If your enemy is hungry,
feed him.
If he is thirsty,
give him a drink.

Don't be conquered by evil,
but overcome evil with good (Rom 12:9-21).

Rom 13

The first part of Romans 13 may be among the most difficult for some Third World women to deal with because it preaches a subjection to authority that has been used through the centuries and is still used to oppress people.

From whatever their tradition or the context of their lived situations, Paul or Paula preaches that "every soul should be subject to the governing authorities" (Rom 13:1). While ordinarily authority is necessary for civil and other kinds of law, such authority has too often been used to deny human dignity, to imprison, to maintain a *status quo* of the rich against the poor, the powerful against the powerless, men against women and children, and the establishment against the marginalized.

Only lately have Third World women recognized that Jesus' view is more out of the tradition of common sense and human dignity. "Give the coin to Caesar if his image is on it, but give to God what is God's" (Matt 22:21; Mark 12:17; Luke 20:25).

What authority belongs to God? What authority comes from God? This is a thorny question which various societies have analyzed in different ways. In the time of Jesus, the Jewish people recognized the difficulties. Herod was "a fox" (Luke 13:32) who had betrayed his Jewish heritage in capitulating to Roman law.

The distinction in differing interpretations of the law partly defined the two groups of the Pharisees and the Sadducees. Some of the Pharisees held to a more legalistic interpretation of the Jewish law. They articulated as many as 613 laws with specific interpretations and applications. It is this group which in the Gospels is often pictured in conflict with Jesus, especially in the interpretation of the law. Jesus argues with their narrow interpretation of laws about the Sabbath, about approved foods, and about uncleanness related to certain persons such as prostitutes and others who are labeled as "sinners."

Another tradition, however, had developed an ethic of love as dominating other considerations. This tradition had been articulated in Exodus, in Deuteronomy, in Jeremiah, in Micah, in others of the prophets, and by many Pharisees. This is the tradition which Jesus had learned and which he articulated over and over in his actions, his teaching, his healing, and his parables.

One striking example is the story of the Prodigal Son. Another example of such compassion is from the Gospel of Luke, the story of the Good Samaritan (Luke 10:30-37) who transcends cultural lines and traditional hatreds, and who embodies common sense and compassion, much as Jesus did.

The Sadducees were representative of and experts in the law and were often called on for official interpretations. Some also are pictured in the Gospels as antagonists of Jesus and as authorities who placed law above persons.

Paul comes from a background different from that of Jesus. Although he is also a Jew, he studied under Hillel and seems to have acquired a more rigid tradition of law and its interpretation. Paul boasts of himself as one very knowledgeable in the law and as one who kept the law strictly for many years, so much so that he first perceived the followers of Jesus as a threat to the law and as persons worthy of imprisonment and persecution.

Moreover, Paul was a Roman citizen who grew up in an urban environment. As such, in contrast to one like Jesus raised in a more rural society, Paul had imbibed a tradition of civil laws in the Roman urban style of order, with authority at the top and with the necessity of obedience to what he considered lawful authority.

In Christ, Paul found not only freedom from the law, but the new law of love. On the opposite side, he was sensitive to criticism of the new Christianity as destructive of civil law and of Roman order. He therefore adopts the Roman ideas of authority coming from God and authorities as being appointed by God (Rom 13:2). This difference between Paul and Jesus will plague Christianity and societies affected by Christianity for all its history.

Paul extends his logic to say that "whoever resists the authority resists the ordinance of God and those who resist will bring judgment on themselves" (Rom 13:2). He makes no distinction here between just and unjust authorities, between just and unjust laws. He does not reflect on the Jesus who was crucified for resisting unjust laws and authorities.

Paul or Paula continues in this uncritical support of authorities by praising them as "God's minister(s)" (Rom 13:4) for good and commending taxes and customs, fear and honor (Rom 13:7) without an acknowledgment of unjust rulers as oppressors who may contradict human dignity and exploit persons.

But the last half of the chapter more reflects the commandment of love which Jesus articulated: "Owe no one anything except to love one another, for the one who loves another has fulfilled the law" (Rom 13:8). The commandments are summed up in this saying: "Love your neighbor as yourself" (Rom 13:9). "Love does no evil to one's neighbor. Therefore love is fulfillment of the law" (Rom 13:10).

Paula calls the followers of Christ to be raised out of sleep. The fullness of time, of being made whole is near. The dawn is coming. "Put on the armor of light" (Rom 13:11-12). Third World women can identify with these admonitions. With Paula they can say: "Let us walk with dignity as in daylight." They reject drunkenness, lust, strife, and envy (Rom 13:13). They put on Christ (Rom 13:14) as they claim their dignity as women, as human persons, as voices for the oppressed and persecuted.

Rom 14

The early Christians had problems with eating food, especially meat, which had been offered to idols. The Roman system was such that most meat had been offered to Roman gods. Christians therefore had a conscience problem. If they ate this meat, were they partaking of a false religion? Some said yes and condemned those who ate it. Others refused to eat it. There were also problems of observing festivals or feast days dedicated to such gods (Rom 14:2-6).

Third World women can face similar problems if they live in a culture where religious food and festivals are part of the life that they do not share. This may be true in parts of India, China, Africa, or South America. In Europe and North America, the conscience problem may be tied in with militarism, uncritical patriotism, exploitation of migrant workers or of those who work in canning, clothing, or other kinds of factories.

Paula calls on all to be strong in a faith that honors and praises God as Lord. Whether living or dying, "we are of the Lord" (Rom 14:8). Christ died and lived again so that he might be Lord of the dead and of the living (Rom 14:8-9).

Like these early Christians, Third World women are not called to judge the consciences of their sisters or brothers (Rom 14:10), but they are called to give an account of themselves to God (Rom 14:12). "The kingdom of God is not eating and drinking, but rightness, peace, and joy in the Holy Spirit" (Rom 14:17). Third World women today, however, often find that in serving Christ, they trust that they are acceptable to God. But whereas Paul says they are also approved by men (Rom 14:18), Third World women often have to take exception, because in standing up for their own dignity and that of others, in standing up for justice and the rights of the poor and marginalized, they are often not only not approved of by men, but for those very actions, they are often condemned and rejected by men, and by some women, too.

With Paula they strive to pursue the things that make for peace and for building up one another. They strive not to offend or scandalize (Rom 14:20). But often they know that speaking out for justice and the rights of the oppressed and marginalized will place them in a position similar to that of Christ who was rejected, condemned, and crucified.

Rom 15

Chapter 15 is a peroration, a summing up and a joyful, prayerful, even ecstatic praising of God, referred to as Father of Christ, and as Holy Spirit. Since this is the last letter we have from Paul, it also serves as a summing up of his ministry to the nations.

Many Third World women struggle to a place of authenticity, where they are not afraid to speak the truth, and where they can fully claim the ministry to which they have been called.

Like Paula, then, they can say that those who are strong have borne and will continue to bear the weaknesses of those who are not strong. Doing that, they have transcended themselves to a place where they no longer need to please themselves (Rom 15:1).

Christ did not live just to please himself but bore the reproaches of others (Rom 15:3). Each is called to build up the good (Rom 15:2). For those things that have been written—the Scriptures, but also the writings of these women from the Third World—are teaching us so that through the patience and strength of these writings we may have hope (Rom 15:4).

These women also pray that the God of patience and of strength may give people one mind with one another according to Christ Jesus (Rom 15:5) so that with one mind and one speech they may give glory to "the God and Father of our Lord Jesus Christ"(Rom 15:6). With Paula they beg people to receive one another as Christ received us to the glory of God (Rom 15:7).

Paula describes Jesus as a minister of the circumcision, that is, of the Jewish covenant, for the truth of God to confirm the promises of the fathers (Rom 15:8) of the Jewish people: Abraham, Moses, and David. Women of the Third World must say that these promises were made not only to the fathers, but also to the mothers, Sarah, Miriam, Michal, and Bathsheba.

But Christ belongs to all the nations. The mercy of God extends to all people. All are called to give glory to

God (Rom 15:9). So do women of the Third World recognize that the cry of freedom belongs to all people. They speak to all nations.

Paula sings:

I will praise your name (Rom 15:9).

Be glad, nations, with all the people (Rom 15:10).

All nations, praise the Lord
and let all the peoples praise her! (Rom 15:11).

Jesus is like a root rising up to lead nations, so much so that nations have hope (Rom 15:12). In a similar way, these women rise up to lead nations so that nations may have hope.

With Paula, these Third World women pray: "Now may the God of hope fill all of you with joy and peace in believing so you may abound in hope by the power of the Holy Spirit" (Rom 15:13).

With Paula, these women say: "Sisters and brothers, I am persuaded that you are full of goodness, you are filled with knowledge, you are able to admonish one another" (Rom 15:14). By speaking this way, they call others to have courage to throw off their oppressions, to claim their leadership and ministry, to speak out so that other hearts can be turned to peace and freedom.

With Paula, they speak boldly and know that it is because of the grace given to them by God (Rom 15:15) so that they can be ministers of Christ Jesus to all the people, offering up the Good News of God, so that all people may be holy to God, through the Holy Spirit (Rom 15:16).

Like Paula, these women know that it is Christ who works in them through word and work, by power of signs and wonders, by power of the Spirit (Rom 15:17-19). Just as Paula preached the Good News from Jerusalem and round about Illyricum (Rom 15:19), so these women speak out in Guatemala, in El Salvador, in South Africa and Kenya, in Korea and India and the Philippines, and indeed even in Australia, North America, and

Europe. They want to preach the Christ of freedom and human dignity where he has not been preached (Rom 15:20-21).

Paula always feels called to new places, even to Rome and Spain (Rom 15:24). However, she will carry a contribution from Macedonia and Greece to the poor of Jerusalem (Rom 15:26).

So, too, these Third World women are called to bridge from one continent to another, from one people to another, to bring contributions from one nation to another—all in the fullness of the blessing of Christ (Rom 15:29).

With Paula, they can pray:

> I call you, sisters and brothers,
> through the Lord Jesus Christ
> and through the love of the Spirit
> to strive with me in prayer
> that we may be delivered
> from those who persecute us
> and come to you in joy
> through the will of God
> that we may rest with you.
> And the God of peace
> be with all of you. Amen (Rom 15:30-33).

Rom 16

At the end of the letter, Paula lists many who have worked with her in her ministry of the Good News. She calls Phoebe her sister who is a minister of the church in Cenchrae (Rom 16:1), the port of Corinth, and she asks that they receive Phoebe in the Lord and stand by her in whatever needs she has, just as she has stood by others.

There are Phoebes in the church of today's Third Worlds. But there are also Priskas and Marys and Tryphosas. What if we substitute the names of some of these Third World women theologians? Then the litany might read:

Greet Maria and Juana, my helpers in Christ Jesus, who have risked their own necks for me. I thank them and all the other groups. And greet those who meet in their house. Greet Rigoberta, my beloved, who is first fruit from Guatemala. Greet Elizabeth, who worked so much for us. Greet Maria Clara and Hilda, my sisters and captives with me, who are notable among the apostles, who indeed were born in Christ before me. Greet Jane and Chung, my beloved in the Lord. Greet Bette, my co-worker and Tamiki, my beloved in the Lord. Greet Thoko and her family. Greet Astrid, chosen in the Lord and Mercy, and the sisters who are with her. Greet one another with a holy kiss. All the churches of Christ greet you (Rom 16:3-16).

Well might Paula speak to the brothers, and sometimes sisters, today to watch out for those who cause division and teachings contrary to the love of Christ. Such ones do not serve Christ, but serve their own bellies, and through oily and flattering speeches deceive the hearts of the simple (Rom 16:17-18).

Paula promises that the God of peace will crush the diabolical soon. She prays that the grace, the gift of our Lord Jesus Christ, may be with them (Rom 16:20). To God is the glory, to the one who is able to establish the Good News of Jesus Christ, the mystery now made manifest to all nations from ages to ages. Amen (Rom 16:25-27).

Recommended Reading

Elliott, Neil. *Liberating Paul: The Justice of God and the Politics of the Apostle.* Maryknoll, N.Y.: Orbis Books, 1994.

Fitzmyer, Joseph A. *According to Paul: Studies in the Theology of the Apostle.* New York: Paulist Press, 1993.

Gillman, Florence M. *Women Who Knew Paul.* Collegeville: The Liturgical Press, 1992.

Meinardus, Otto F. A. *St. Paul in Greece.* Athens, Greece: Lycabettus Press, 1989.

Penna, Romano. *Paul the Apostle: Jew and Greek Alike.* Collegeville: The Liturgical Press, 1996.

Richards, Hubert. *The Gospel According to St. Paul.* Collegeville: The Liturgical Press, 1991.

Swidler, Leonard, et al. *Bursting the Bonds? A Jewish-Christian Dialogue on Jesus and Paul.* Maryknoll, N.Y.: Orbis Books, 1990.